So
You
Want
to Be
a
MEDIUM?

About the Author

Reverend Rose Vanden Eynden (Ohio) has been a spiritual student all of her life. At sixteen, she began reading tarot cards, and she became a professional consultant in her early twenties. She holds a bachelor of science in education and has been a licensed massage therapist since 1996. Rose started studying mediumship in 1997, and in 2000 she became a certified medium with the Indiana Association of Spiritualists and an ordained Spiritualist minister with the United Spiritualists of the Christ Light Church, of which she is a founding member. Rose lives in Cincinnati, and *So You Want to Be a Medium?* is her first book. Find out more about the author at www.vanden eynden.biz.

So You Want to Be a MEDIUM?

A Down-to-Earth Guide

Rose Vanden Eynden

Llewellyn Publications
Woodbury, Minnesota

First Edition
First Printing, 2006

Book design and layout by Joanna Willis
Cover design by Lisa Novak
Cover background images © Artville
Interior illustration by Llewellyn art department

The publisher and author gratefully acknowledge Reverend Terry Ryan for permission to use his name and the ideas and words contained in his lecture "Natural Law," 2000.

Llewellyn is a registered trademark of Llewellyn Worldwide, Ltd.

Library of Congress Cataloging-in-Publication Data
Eynden, Rose Vanden.
    So you want to be a medium? : a down-to-Earth guide / Rose Vanden Eynden.— 1st ed.
        p. cm.
    Includes bibliographical references and index.
    ISBN-13: 978-0-7387-0856-0
    ISBN-10: 0-7387-0856-9
      1. Mediums. I. Title.

BF1286.E96 2006
133.9'1—dc22   2005057775

Llewellyn Publications
A Division of Llewellyn Worldwide, Ltd.
2143 Wooddale Drive, Dept. 0-7387-0856-9
Woodbury, MN 55125-2989, U.S.A.
www.llewellyn.com

Printed in the United States of America

Contents

List of Exercises and Meditations   *xi*

Acknowledgments   *xv*

Introduction   *xvii*

Part 1: Starting from Scratch

1 Defining Terms   5

2 Modern Spiritualism   9

3 Natural Law   15

Part 2: Preparation of the Mind and Body

4 I Want to Be a Medium When I Grow Up   31

5 The Five Senses   35

6 Discernment   39

7 Physical versus Spiritual Awareness   43

8 Auras and Chakras   47

9 Breathing   57

10 Meditation   59

Part 3: Who's Who in the Spirit World

11 Joy Guides   79

12 Protector Guides   83

13 Doctor Teachers   91

14 Doctor Chemists   95

15 Master Guides   103

16 Ascended Masters   111

17 Angels   115

18 Outer Band Guides   117

19 Sorting It All Out   121

20 Guides of a Different Nature   127

Part 4: Digging In

21 Roll Call   135

22 Focus   139

23 Symbolism   145

24 Dreams and Dreamwork   163

25 Other Exercises and Tasks   173

26 The Games Spirit People Play   179

27 Questions? I Got Questions!   185

28 Putting It All Together   189

29 Reach Out, Touch Spirit   195

Part 5: Readings and Sittings

30 A Few Words about Divination Tools   203

31 The Victim   207

32 Introductions   211

33 The Messages   217

34 Look Who's Talking   221

35 The Don't List   225

36 Some Tips about Evidence   229

37 Broaching the Subject of Death   233

38 Ending a Reading   235

Conclusion: Where to Go from Here   239
Appendix A: The Principles of Spiritualism   243
Appendix B: Spiritualist Organizations in the United States   245
Bibliography   247
Index   249

Exercises and Meditations

White Light Meditation 41

To See Auras 48

To Feel Auras 48

Chakra Interpretation Quiz 52

Deep-Breathing Exercise 58

Simple Relaxation Meditation 62

Simple Protection Meditation 63

Chakra-Cleansing Meditation 65

Concentration Meditation #1: The Ball 68

Concentration Meditation #2: Many Balls 68

Concentration Meditation #3: Word Meditation 69

Special Place Meditation 70

Guide Meditation 100

Master Guide Meditation 109

Symbol Exercise #1 149

Symbol Exercise #2: The Weather Report 157

Symbol Exercise #3: The Stock Market 160

Symbol Exercise #4: First Call 161

Dream Exercise #1: Contact with a Loved One 167

Dream Exercise #2: Going to School 169

Dream Exercise #3: Assistance, Please 170
Joy Guide Exercise: Ask and You Shall Receive 174
Protector Exercise: Point Me in the Right Direction 175
Doctor Teacher Exercise: Finding Information 176
Doctor Chemist Exercise: Tour Guide 177
Game #1: It's All in the Cards 179
Game #2: Color My World 180
Game #3: The Name Game 181
Symbol Interpretation Quiz 189
Master Teacher Exercise: Connecting with Ascended Masters . 196
Divination Tool Blessing 204

This book is lovingly dedicated to my mother,
Frances Klein Finley,
who passed into spirit on May 10, 2000.
Mom, keep the light on for me, will you?

Acknowledgments

No one completes a task like writing a book without help. Writing may be a solitary business, but there are always people in the wings who encourage you, who ask the right questions, and who generally make your life more livable as you struggle for words. For these reasons, and many more, I need to acknowledge the following people:

My online writing groups, Quill and Ink and Beyond the Sea, which have been so supportive of my endeavors. Special thanks and love to Kimberly Aldrich, Lisa Alvarado, Char Chaffin, Jay Fox, Sallie Johnson-Wellbrock, Meridy Migchelbrink, Kevin Saito, Toniann Scime, and Stephanie Siria. No one could ask for better friends.

All of the instructors at Camp Chesterfield in Indiana, in particular Reverend A. Win Srogi and Reverend Terry Ryan, for their notes and insights regarding Natural Law, and Reverend Shirley Srogi, for her information about symbolism. Extra special thanks to my first development teacher, Reverend Daniel Dunham, for his patience and friendship. These dedicated people willingly passed their knowledge on to me, and I will always be grateful beyond words.

My spiritual allies, with whom I am able to share experiences: Reverend Judy Brooks, Reverend Jane DeVore, Reverend Jaccolin Franchina, Joanne Franchina, Reverend Susan Hill, Christine Sabick,

Jill Sandy, and Reverend Dan Wegert. Thank you for making the journey with me and for all the laughter along the way.

The United Spiritualists of the Christ Light Church community, especially Alison Dunham, Reverend Barbara Dunham, Earl Dunham, Ron Clough, Reverend John Hein, and the late Theresa Mayhugh. You have brought more light to my life than you can possibly know.

The students who have touched my life in so many ways over the years. I always say that I learn just as much from my students as they learn from me. Thank you for your open minds and hearts.

My friends, who may not share my beliefs but who never cease to remind me that everything is connected in a circle of love and respect: Kristy DuSablon, Tom Mattingly, Marilyn Meyer, Pam Miller, Holly Sauerbrunn, Tracy Schoster, Michelle White, and especially Melissa Edwards.

My family, who see through eyes of love no matter what I do, especially my sons, Max and Ben, and my husband, Keith.

And finally, my spirit teachers, who keep me on the straight and narrow. I know you're there; I feel you every day. I hope I make you proud.

ROSE VANDEN EYNDEN

Introduction

So you want to be a medium. Let me see if I can guess what piqued your interest in this unusual concept of communicating with the dead.

Perhaps you've seen the famous mediums on television, and you've watched them connect audience members with their loved ones who've passed over to the Other Side. Maybe you've thought, "Wow! That's pretty amazing. I wonder what it would be like to talk to people in Spirit."

Possibly you've lost someone close to you—a parent, spouse, or friend—and you've been missing that person terribly. And maybe a few nights ago, as you sat thinking about your dear one, you suddenly caught a whiff of his pipe tobacco or her favorite perfume in the air. The thought crossed your mind: "Was that . . . ?" As it did, you realized you truly hoped that your special someone could still feel your love.

Or perhaps, not too long ago, you dreamt of a place of intense beauty and permeating peace. In your dream, the colors around you pulsed with a radiance you'd never seen before. The flowers that grew in the rolling fields filled the air with a lush, rich scent, and everything emanated a light, an energy, that consumed you from head to toe with a satisfying sensation of perfection. Your dream ended much too soon, and you found yourself longing to dream of that place again.

Does any of this sound familiar? I can't tell you how many of my students and clients have described situations similar to these that have compelled them to seek answers about the reality of survival after death and the veracity of after-death communication. These folks come to my office, my church, or my classes searching for truth, and many of them leave convinced that the afterlife, and communication with those in that world, are as real as the book you are holding in your hands. It is my hope and my fervent prayer that by reading this book, you too will find some of the answers you need.

This book has been organized and written with you in mind. I'm not going to pretend there aren't other books about mediumship on the market today. I am personally thrilled by the surge in attention that after-death communication and mediumship are currently receiving. However, it's been my experience that many of the other books out there focus on relating transcripts of personal sittings to their readers, using these to prove the reality and truth of after-death communication. While these can be fascinating to follow, I wanted to write something different. I wanted to pass on the knowledge of Spirit that I have acquired so it might help people to understand what a wonderful and enlightening experience it is to have Spirit play a prevalent role in your life. Yes, there are stories in this book, but hopefully they are stories that help to illustrate specific points and give specific information that Spirit is trying to highlight for you through me.

The purpose of this book is simple: to introduce you, the reader, to the marvelous spirit world and to show you how building a relationship with those in Spirit can enhance your life. Living with Spirit is really what being a medium is all about. After many years of working with those in the spirit world, I can tell you that my life has irrevocably changed. I am happier and more focused than I ever have been. This kind of positive change can happen for you, too. I hope that you'll find a difference for yourself in these pages, in your relationships with those you meet in Spirit, and within your own heart, where all change ultimately takes place.

So are you ready to get started? Terrific! Let's begin, then, by saying a prayer. We pray, of course, to our Divine Creator, God or Goddess, Infinite Intelligence—whatever name you call that pervading presence that fills our hearts and our lives with peace and love. Sometimes people get confused and think mediums are advocating praying to our guides, our deceased loved ones, or our guardian angels. This is not the case. All of these helpers in the spirit world were given to us by Creator, and all glory, honor, and thanksgiving for their help must be given to that Divine Source. Spirit encourages us (in reality, demands of us!) to have a deep connection to God. Prayer, of course, helps us to make that connection. Prayer also helps to build a positive energy vibration around all that we do, and since we are embarking on a new and exciting adventure, it's probably a good idea to have some help from the higher realms as we do so. As you read this prayer, either aloud or in your mind, concentrate on the words and their meanings. The more energy you put into a prayer, the more you will get back from it.

Great Creator,

I ask for Your blessing as I begin this journey toward enlightenment. I ask that You guide me throughout this process and that You open my mind and heart to the wisdom presented to me. Please help me to find the messages that You wish me to know as I make my way through these pages, and allow me to comprehend the intrinsic love that resides within You and Your ways. In the holiest name, I pray. Amen.

Now turn the page, and see what Spirit has in store for you!

Part 1

STARTING
from
SCRATCH

So what exactly are we talking about when we say the word *mediumship*? Because there are so many different sources available today and so many different meanings ascribed to the words that we use, I think a good way to start this book is by defining our terms. More than likely, we are discussing the very same issues, situations, and experiences. Semantics, however, often has a way of building roadblocks to understanding rather than helping people to communicate better. Let's talk first about some different terminology that will be used throughout this book, so that we're all starting with the same information.

1 Defining Terms

A *medium* is someone who is sensitive to the vibrations of the spirit world and can communicate with entities there. This person may also relate messages from those in the spirit world to those here in the physical world. A medium is different from a psychic. The difference between the two hinges on the concept of *spirit contact*. A *psychic* picks up her impressions through ESP, or extrasensory perception. She may also utilize telepathy, or a mind-to-mind link with the person for whom she reads (although the psychic may or may not be aware of this method of retrieving information). A medium gets his information directly from Spirit. He may communicate with his client's loved ones who have passed, or information may come from his client's spirit guides. This direct link makes the information very accurate and reliable. I believe that many psychics receive their impressions from their own spirit guides but just don't realize it. They would probably enhance their readings immeasurably if they learned how to work more closely with their spirit people.

Now, just a side note: please don't take this comparison between psychics and mediums as some sort of one-upsmanship. There are many talented psychics working today who are not mediums, and I am not suggesting that they all need to become mediums to be better professionals. I can only speak from my own experience, which illuminates for me how much more accurate the readings I have done for my own clients have been since I've learned to work with Spirit in my practice. Everyone must follow the path that is right for his or her own individual progression. Becoming a medium was the way to go for me; it might not be for everyone. For you, however, who have picked up this book to learn more about communicating with Spirit, let's move on.

Mediumship, then, can be defined as the process by which a medium establishes contact with an entity in the spirit world and communicates with that entity. The entities in the spirit world can be human, as in the case of passed loved ones and spirit guides, or a medium may contact angels, animal energies (such as beloved pets), and elemental energies (such as faeries). *After-death communication* can be included under the umbrella of mediumship, for it refers specifically to the process of communicating with someone who has experienced the change called death and dwells now on the Other Side.

Summerland is one of the myriad terms used to describe what people experience after they transition from their physical life. In this book, we will refer to the afterlife as Summerland, the Other Side, the spirit world, and possibly other names. *Summerland* comes from the Welsh *Gwlad Yr Haf,* which translates into "the Land of Summer" and is the origin of the Wiccan term for the *otherworld* (Spiral Dance 2004). Summerland is all around us here in the physical plane, but most of the time, we cannot see it or sense it in any way. This is because everything in the spirit world vibrates energetically at a much higher rate than we do in our plane of existence. Higher vibrations cannot be seen with the naked eye, nor can they be picked up using the normal senses of hearing, touch, taste, sight, and smell. Occasionally, we are able to tap into the spirit world, often when we're not even trying. Have you ever seen movement out of the corner of your eye, but when you turned to look in that direction, you saw nothing at all? More than likely, you just saw a spirit moving past you in Summerland. When we as mediums work with Spirit, we have to heighten our vibrations to hear, see, or sense them. We'll talk more about that process later in the book. Summerland, though, is a wonderful place, and we can learn to have access to those who dwell there, like our passed loved ones and spirit guides.

Spirit guides are the people in Spirit who work with us, performing a variety of duties. We have at least five main spirit guides. Before our current incarnation, while we were still in Summerland, these particular guides agreed to aid us while we took on another lifetime. As we grow spiritually during our physical incarnation, our guides grow spiritually on the Other Side. They are our closest companions, and they will be with us until we make our transition to Summerland, where they will meet us again. We'll discuss all of our different guides at length in Part Three, "Who's Who in the Spirit World."

Spirit (with a capital *S*) is a catch-all way to refer to those who dwell in Summerland, as well as a word that highlights belief in Creator. When a medium mentions communicating with Spirit or being led by Spirit, he is acknowledging the influences of his spirit guides and teachers, his passed loved ones, and his connection and faith in a higher power. Most people refer to this divine presence as God. Some people, though, are uncomfortable with that term because of its connotation of God as a male entity. I prefer a more general, gender-neutral term, which is why I personally refer to that divinity as Creator most of the time. In Spiritualism, many mediums and ministers prefer the term *Mother-Father God* to remind us that within Creator we find both male and female energies. Creator is the ultimate source of balance; it only makes sense that Creator holds both of these energies within Itself. Spiritualist mediums will often refer directly to Spirit, as we believe that Creator gave us Spirit to help us in our everyday matters as well as to guide us ever closer to the source of ultimate love and goodness in the Universe.

A *Spiritualist* is one who believes, as the basis of his or her religion, in the communication between this world and the spirit world by means of mediumship and who endeavors to behave in accordance with the highest teachings derived from this communication. *Spiritualism* is a science, a philosophy, and a religion of continuous life, based upon the demonstrated fact of communication by means of mediumship with those who live in the spirit world (National Spiritualist Association of Churches 2002, 35). A person does not have to be a Spiritualist to be a medium, nor does she have to convert to Spiritualism in order to practice or believe in spirit communication. Many of the world's great religions have elements of spirit communication prevalent in them. In Jewish tradition, the Kaballah is studied as a mystical connection to Creator. The Christian Bible is filled with instances of prophecy, healing, and other spirit phenomena. The Muslim religion is based upon the Koran, which was given to the prophet Mohammed by the angel Gabriel. The Pagan traditions have many connections to ancient, esoteric mystery schools, which highlight divination, prophecy, and healing. Many Eastern philosophies, like Hinduism and Buddhism, endorse the idea of reincarnation. Most major religions teach a belief in an afterlife and encourage their followers to work hard to ensure a place there after this lifetime. A belief in mediumship and communication with those in the spirit world doesn't seem too out of place next to these faiths and their systems.

Although a person does not have to be a Spiritualist in order to practice or believe in mediumship, the interest in after-death communication and the proof of its reality began with Modern Spiritualism in the United States. In the next chapter, we'll take a few moments to discuss the birth of this movement and its repercussions, which are still felt throughout the world today.

2   Modern Spiritualism

Modern Spiritualism began on March 31, 1848, in the small, quiet town of Hydesville, New York. So what happened on that March evening that so changed the perception of people about the spirit world?

The movement of Spiritualism can be traced to a house owned by Margaret and John Fox, who moved into the home in December of 1847. The Foxes had an older son, David, who lived on his own farm, as well as three daughters. Leah, the eldest, was not present that evening, although she later became a famous medium. Margaretta, also called Maggie, and Catherine, also called Katie, were home on the night of March 31, along with their parents. The incidents that incited the birth of Spiritualism are recounted in *Hydesville in History*, by M. E. Cadwallader.

Through most of their stay in the house, the family had heard noises that they couldn't explain. In January 1848, the noises became knockings, sometimes heard in the bedroom, sometimes heard in the cellar. The rappings often caused tremors throughout the house. During the month of February, the knockings became so distinct and continuous that the family had a hard time resting at night. Of course, they tried to pinpoint the cause of the knocks, but they could only ascertain that the noises came from inside the house. No other cause could be found. Other phenomena also manifested, such as Katie feeling a cold hand upon her brow; an invisible presence, like a dog, that settled on the bed one night; and the pulling of the covers off the bed as well.

On Friday, March 31, 1848, the family, weary from so many sleepless nights and countless investigations into what was causing the trouble, retired early. They had moved all their beds into one room, and of course the knockings started as soon as they tried to sleep. The girls, whose exact ages are disputed but who were most likely young adolescents at the time, were more excited than alarmed by the noises, and they chattered away about them even though their mother tried to keep them silent.

Finally, after a long while listening to the knocks, Katie, the youngest, sat up in bed and said, "Here, Mr. Split-foot, do as I do." She proceeded to make a number of silent gestures in the air; their effect was instantaneous. The invisible rapper immediately knocked a corresponding number of times, to indicate that her movements had been seen. Katie, delighted with this new game, cried, "Only look, mother! It can see as well as hear." Obviously, the invisible knocker was attempting to communicate.

Mrs. Fox, then, addressed it: "Count ten." Ten raps sounded. She then asked the invisible rapper to indicate the ages of first Maggie and then Katie. The correct number of knocks, corresponding to each girl's age, were given; apparently, this being had intelligence as well.

Mrs. Fox continued her questioning, and the rappings made in response correctly answered each of her inquiries. Finally, she asked, "Are you a man?" She received no response to this question. When she countered with "Are you a spirit?" a series of very firm knocks was made.

It was determined through subsequent communications that the spirit was a traveling peddler named Charles B. Rosna, who had been murdered by the former occupants of the Fox family home.

Many years later, a full skeleton was discovered in a wall of the cellar, just where Mr. Rosna's spirit told the family it would be.

Naturally, when word got out about the Fox family home, interested seekers began to flock there. Immature and impressionable as they were, the Fox sisters were overwhelmed by the publicity they received, since the spirit seemed willing to communicate only when they were present. The spirit also followed them wherever they went, as the girls were sent to live in other places to escape the attention they were receiving. When someone finally thought to ask about this, the following message was spelled out to them:

> Dear friends, you must proclaim this truth to the world. This is the dawning of a new era; you must not try to conceal it any longer. When you do your duty God will protect you and good spirits will watch over you. (Fodor 1934)

Thus the message of Spiritualism, and its advent as a new spiritual movement, was born.

The girls began to appear at public demonstrations, where they would communicate with the spirit world before a live audience, and the fascination with spirit phenomena grew. More and more people became interested in their own mediumship development, and mediums sprang up all across the United States. Home circles and séances became all the rage. Even Mary Todd Lincoln, the first lady of the United States, held séances in the White House, which her husband, President Abraham Lincoln, also attended.

For the Fox sisters, however, the revelation of spirit phenomena was a mixed blessing. None of the sisters handled the fame, or the responsibility of bearing spirit messages to the hungry masses, very well. All of the girls married, but their personal lives were plagued by the pressures of a demanding public. After a terrible quarrel and a vow to ruin their sister Leah, Maggie gave a public lecture in New York in which she denounced Spiritualism and claimed that she had produced the famous rappings at will, demonstrating this for the crowd. Her sister Katie supported her, and they revealed the ways in which they claimed they'd deceived the public.

This confession, however, did nothing to quell the rising popularity of the movement, and a year later, Maggie retracted her statements, claiming that she was in desperate financial straits and needed the money she'd received from the lecture. Dr. Isaac Funk, a well-known American publisher, once said of Maggie, "For five dollars, she would have denied her mother and sworn to anything" (Fodor 1934).

The irony of Maggie's love-hate relationship with her spiritual gifts was apparent at the end of her life in 1905, when she was attended by a female doctor called Mrs. Mellen. During her last days, Mrs. Mellen cared for Maggie in a tiny, dirty room, one with no closets or hiding spaces. Maggie was unable to move her hands or her feet, and yet, when she asked questions of her spirit guides, they rapped out the answers on the floor, walls, and ceiling of the room, a phenomenon Mrs. Mellen witnessed. Will we ever really know the complete truth about Maggie Fox and her mediumship? Probably not, but the fact remains that she was able to demonstrate honest and proven spirit phenomena under the strictest of test conditions. Her personal life and all of her mistakes are, as is true for all of us, between her and Creator.

Both Katie and Leah Fox were also tested and declared legitimate by some of the greatest scientists and thinkers of their time. Although none of the sisters led exemplary lives, who among us can cast the first stone? Remember, they were the first to experience such contact in the terms by which we understand it today. They were the epicenter of a phenomenal spiritual movement that shook the foundations of many long-established religious views. I agree with the findings of Nandor Fodor in his article "The Ghost Story which Started Spiritualism": it's hard to imagine that children could have schemed together to begin and perpetuate such an elaborate fraud.

Are there fraudulent mediums? Of course there are. They existed at the beginning of Modern Spiritualism, and they exist today. Don't be too quick to dismiss all mediums, however, just because of a few deceitful ones. There are dishonest people in every profession, from sports figures to CEOs of large corporations to cashiers who steal from their own tills. Does this mean that every person who serves in that occupation is corrupt? Of course it doesn't. The same can be said of mediums, too.

Spiritualism has survived many trials and much skepticism to remain alive and vital in the world today. Centers of Spiritualist phenomena and education, like Lily Dale Assembly in New York and Camp Chesterfield in Indiana, continue to thrive as more and more people become interested in exploring the idea of after-death communication and their relationships with those in the spirit world. The National Spiritualist Association of Churches (NSAC) is the oldest and largest organization devoted to the religion of Spiritualism in the United States, founded on September 27, 1893. The NSAC estimates that there are around four thousand practicing Spiritualists in the United States today, although because so many people do not declare this religion but practice its belief, the number of supporters of Spiritualism is hard to establish.

As a religion, Spiritualism embodies beliefs in several tenets in conjunction with mediumship. Spiritualists believe in *Infinite Intelligence,* a way of describing God without the male/female connotations that most religions place on Creator. Spiritualists are also very concerned with the idea of personal responsibility and do not, like some faiths, believe in vicarious atonement. In other words, Spiritualists believe that each one of us is solely responsible for our own actions and that no savior can take on our sins or transgressions for us. We all have free will and must choose our actions reasonably and responsibly. Spiritualists believe very strongly in the Natural Laws of the Universe (which we will discuss in the next section), and one Natural Law is that of cause and effect. Whatever you do will return to you in some way, whether in this lifetime or in the next. The idea that a savior can remove your responsibility for your actions does not make sense to Spiritualists, because it violates this Natural Law of the Universe.

As I mentioned before, one does not have to be a Spiritualist to be a medium, nor does one need to leave a current religious practice in order to include spirit communication in that belief system. I found the religion of Spiritualism to be the right choice for me. Its principles and beliefs made sense to me, and it fit in well with my study and background in Wicca and magick as well. I also could reconcile within Spiritualism my own thoughts and feelings about Jesus, held over from my Roman Catholic upbringing, and I could still study and use the Christian Bible along with other religious texts as a basis for further growth and enlightenment. Since I was also studying to be a medium, it seemed that Spirit was once again leading me to something that I needed in my life. When I began training at Camp Chesterfield in Indiana in 1997, I never imagined I would someday become an ordained Spiritualist minister. When Spirit calls you, you can dig in your heels and ignore that call all you like, but take it from me: Spirit won't leave you alone until you face the music and determine what your choice is.

Perhaps this short discussion of Spiritualism will spur some of you on to explore it as a religion, science, and philosophy, and perhaps its tenets will resonate for you. If so, the appendices and bibliography in this book may be a good place for you to start. They include many excellent sources relating to Spiritualism. For now, let's move on in our discussion of mediumship.

3 Natural Law

The foundations of mediumship and after-death communication cannot be complete without some mention of Natural Law. Just as there are laws governing our nation that all people are expected to follow, there are Natural Laws of the Universe that all human beings, and all of nature, adhere to as well. Natural Law oversees all that has been created, and Natural Law has been set in motion by God. It can be thought of as "God in action in the Universe" (Ryan 2000). Natural Law is immutable; it never changes or varies. These laws are constants in the Universe.

In searching for information about Natural Law, I discovered that there are many sources discussing it, and the names and numbers of the laws vary from source to source. Is this because the laws themselves change? No, I don't believe so. It is obvious to me that this is so because the perceptions and understandings of the authors of these texts vary, and this is reflected in their work. Does that make the laws themselves flawed? No. Natural Law comes from God, so it cannot in any way be flawed. The only flaws come from our misunderstandings concerning the laws. We are human beings, so we can only speak about things from our own levels of experience and comprehension. This means that sometimes our interpretations of the laws may not be as deep or as encompassing as they should be. We are all learning and growing. Each of us is personally responsible for learning about the laws and working with them in accordance with our understanding. Just as in society, ignorance of the law does not mean that we don't have to live by it.

I am explaining this to you here for a reason. I have chosen to highlight only some of the Natural Laws of the Universe in this book. I was guided to discuss these particular laws because they are essential to an understanding of mediumship. Other laws do exist, and if you are interested in learning more about Natural Law, I encourage you to pursue the study on your own. And remember, my interpretation and understanding of the laws may also be flawed. I'm human, too. I can only give to you what has been given to me and tested through my own experience. You can draw your own conclusions based upon your own tests.

Underlying Principles of Natural Law

By realizing that the Universe operates under Natural Law, we begin to understand that it is thus always operating in perfect order and harmony. Even in the midst of chaos, the Universe is still running due to the control of Natural Law. Natural Law influences and defines all aspects of life, in this lifetime, in eternity, and in all planes of existence. According to Natural Law, our ordinary state of being is good. We feel happy. Our world moves in an orderly fashion. "Good" equates to everything that encourages unity in the Universe—that is, unity in God. Evil can be seen, then, as everything that separates us from God.

Natural Law applies to everyone and everything. No one can escape its influence. This means that justice will come to all people, either here or hereafter. Does this negate a belief in free will? Not at all. It simply means that when we live in accordance with Natural Law, we have absolute control over our lives. We help ourselves, we help others, and we help our world. Natural Law provides for us a way to avoid negative outcomes and circumstances. We are still given a choice: to work with the law or to work against it. This is why a better understanding of Natural Law is helpful in every way, including in our study of mediumship.

Natural Law #1: The Law of Love

In *Good News Bible*'s Gospel of Matthew, chapter 22, verses 34–40, Jesus is approached by one of the teachers of Jewish Law, who asks him:

> "Which is the greatest commandment in the law?" Jesus answered, " 'Love the Lord your God with all your heart, with all your soul, and with all your mind.' This is the greatest and the most important commandment. The second most important commandment is like it: 'Love your neighbor as you love yourself.' The whole Law of Moses and the teachings of the prophets depend on these two commandments."

This passage illustrates the most important Natural Law: the Law of Love. In these two aspects of love, loving God and loving humanity (including ourselves!), we find the basis for all the other laws of the Universe. The love exemplified in this law, however, is love in its purest and most potent form. It is love without conditions and restrictions. It is love that purifies us by freeing us from jealousy, negativity, and revenge. It is transcendent and yet still attainable by all those who strive to achieve it.

Paraphrased as "Do for others what you want them to do for you" (Matthew 7:12), this tenet is also known as the golden rule. This is an example of how Natural Law is truly universal throughout humanity. The golden rule appears in many different cultures and spiritual traditions. It may be worded in a different way, but its basic message is always the same.

The Law of Love is the basic foundation for everything within Natural Law. Without love, we drift further away from the Source of All, God, Creator, Infinite Intelligence. With love, we move ever closer to that source, becoming more powerful than anything we can possibly imagine.

Natural Law #2: The Law of Mind

In *The Kybalion: A Study of the Hermetic Philosophy of Ancient Egypt and Greece,* the first of the seven Hermetic principles is the Principle of Mentalism. This law states, "The All is Mind; the Universe is mental." The great truth of this law is that everything is consciousness. Everything that is visible and apparent to us, as well as all that is invisible and unnoticed, is Spirit—the "Universal, Infinite, Living Mind" (1912, 26–27). We exist within the ever-continuing Mind of God. We are Spirit, and we are connected to everything else that exists within our Universe. Within this law, we can see and begin to understand the separation of our mind into two sections: the lower mind, which controls and runs our everyday lives and is greatly affected by ego, and the higher mind, which is directly linked to the Divine Source (Ryan 2000). As human beings, we are in a constant state of struggle to bring the lower mind into accordance and harmony with the higher mind. One way to do this is to silence the lower mind, which can be achieved through meditation. We will talk more about meditation later in the book, but it is a key to successful work as a medium and is one of the best ways to access our own higher selves and the other realms of the Universe. To do this, we must master the Law of Mind.

Natural Law #3: The Law of Vibration

If we understand the Law of Mind, we can begin to see how all matter is spiritual energy moving at different rates of vibration. No two things are identical, no matter how much they may seem to be, because at the most basic level, they have their own unique vibrations. For example, my sons are identical twins. Many people have a hard time figuring out ways to keep straight who is who. Folks will often ask me, "How do you tell Max and Ben apart?" Aside from their slight physical differences (one is a bit taller and has bigger feet, and one has a rounder face), I usually chuckle to myself when I prepare to answer this question. Anyone who is around my boys long enough will start to instinctively sense the differences between the two. At a very basic energy level, one moves at a much slower pace than the other. Of course, this is not the only difference between my boys, but do they vibrate at different rates? You betcha, and it's easy to see when you spend just five minutes with them. We all have our own unique rate of vibration, as this law describes.

To better understand the idea of energy vibration, think for a moment about how you feel on a spring day. Have you ever noticed how everything in the world seems right on a bright, sunny morning? Imagine standing outside, looking up at the azure sky unmarred by a single cloud. Notice the sun's light pressing its warm fingers against your skin. Take a deep breath and feel the vitality of the sweet, clear air coursing through you. You feel alive, filled with vigor, ready to take on any challenges that come your way. You may even feel physically better than you have in ages: a walk in the park or a lap around the block may suddenly become quite attractive. You have more energy than you remember having all winter.

Yes, that's right—your *energy vibration* has heightened, and you didn't even realize it!

Now think about how you feel on a rainy, cold day. When you look out your window, the sky is gunmetal gray, filled with clouds and a steady drizzle. The dampness seems to permeate everything, enveloping you in its chilly embrace. You feel tired, grumpy, and unwilling to do anything except curl up on the couch under a warm blanket. You're drained of any ambition you had for the day.

Exactly—your energy vibration has significantly dropped.

Now think about our loved ones and guides who dwell on the Other Side. Many sources indicate that Summerland is a beautiful place, practically indescribable in our limited terms, but so much more astounding than even our most exquisite landmarks here on earth. They don't call it Summerland for nothing! Imagine living in such an astonishing place. No wonder our spirit friends' energy vibrations are so high: they are alive in ways we can scarcely imagine. They are also much closer to the Divine Source of all energy—Creator—when they are in Summerland. Their energy vibration is constantly high.

In working with those in Summerland, we learn that this energy vibration is much higher and faster than the rate of vibration that we have here on the physical plane. In order to communicate with Spirit, a medium must raise his rate of vibration. Our spirit guides or loved ones must lower their rates of vibration so that we can meet somewhere in the middle to make a connection.

Think about the propeller on an airplane. When the plane is flying, the propeller is moving so fast that the naked eye cannot see it. Yet this movement propels the plane forward so that it can travel from one place to another. When the plane lands and the pilot shuts down the engine, the propeller slows, making it visible to any people who happen to be around. This is what Spirit must do to communicate with a medium—slow down its vibration. The medium must speed up his vibration as much as possible so that it is more likely that the connection to Spirit will be made. We will address ways to heighten our energy vibrations for message work later in this book. This is the reason, however, that we say that the Law of Vibration governs mediumship: without the connection of energy vibrations, communication with the spirit world could not take place.

Natural Law #4: The Law of Attraction

Once we understand that everything in the Universe vibrates at a distinct energetic rate, we can also realize that these energies have an affinity for and are attracted to similar energies. The old adage "Like attracts like" fits into this Natural Law. In our social lives, we often find ourselves in groups of people who share similar interests, like sports or other hobbies. Many of us attend a certain church because we feel the need to share our spiritual experiences with others who believe in the same tenets that we do. Likewise, our spirit guides and teachers connect with us because we have similarities with them. For example, I have an interest in magickal training, and two of my spirit guides claim this same background. Many times, we've shared a physical incarnation with our guides, and we may still have an affinity for that particular time in history, whether it be ancient Egyptian or Renaissance British. Our similar energies keep us together and help to bind us to our guides. This is an example of the Law of Attraction in action.

The Law of Attraction also goes hand in hand with the Law of Mind. The Law of Attraction splits the thinking process into two: desire and expectation (Ryan 2000). The Law of Mind tells us that all is consciousness. The Law of Attraction teaches us that we should desire nothing we do not expect to get and that we should never expect anything that we do not want. When we put these two laws into action and we focus our expectation on something specific that we desire, we then become irresistible and the Law of Attraction brings to us that which we desired and expected. Again, the saying "Be careful what you wish for, because you just might get it" is much more than an old wives' tale when we understand how Natural Law applies. This is positive thinking in its most powerful and influential state. The other side of this coin is, of course, the dreadful effects that negative thinking can bring to us. We are capable of drawing to us the very things that we most fear by constantly seeing them, in our mind's eye, as invading our lives. Make no mistake: the Law of Attraction will bring you negative situations if that is what you choose to dwell upon in your mind. Again, this is potent proof of the Law of Mind in action through the Law of Attraction.

Natural Law #5: The Law of Cause and Effect

The next Natural Law is another extension of laws already addressed. The Law of Cause and Effect states that every action has an appropriate reaction. This law demands that we accept personal responsibility for everything in our lives, as we are constantly creating causes that result in effects. There are no chance occurrences in life; all is in Divine Order, and every action brings a result that is correct for it. If our lives are not what we would like them to be, we have the power to change them by changing what we are doing to create our circumstances.

Change begins at the most basic level: in our minds. The Law of Mind states that everything is consciousness. The Law of Vibration and the Law of Attraction both tell us that thoughts are things, and thoughts create their own vibrations and draw to us that which we ask for. To make important changes in our lives, we must first begin by changing our thoughts and our attitudes. If we are constantly complaining that we have no money, what are we drawing to ourselves? The very limited financial situation that we are lamenting! Remember, like attracts like. The Law of Cause and Effect takes the Law of Attraction one step further. If we need more money in our lives, we need to think in a productive and profitable way. We need to change something (cause) to bring about the desired end (effect). We always have the power to change. Our biggest hurdle is usually recognizing how much power we really do have to make changes.

The Law of Cause and Effect has another law that extends from it—the Law of Compensation. This law justly metes out payment to us for all of our actions, whether they be good, bad, or indifferent. Simply put, this law states that we receive back from the Universe what we give out. We might not always receive it right away; it may take days, months, years, or lifetimes to receive payment for some actions. But the justified compensation will always come at some point.

The Law of Cause and Effect is an important one in mediumship because it reinforces how important it is to do our work in the world with love and compassion. Setting our intentions before we do any type of work is essential to reaping positive benefits from our actions. If we work in love and ask that our work be blessed, then we will only affect our clients, ourselves, and our world in positive ways. This is important whether we are professional mediums, construction workers, garbage collectors, parents, or anything else. Remember, Natural Law is about bringing us closer to divinity, and to do that, we must live in love. All else separates us from God.

Natural Law #6: The Law of Balance

The Law of Balance justifies equilibrium in all things. All actions, no matter what their nature, must be balanced. As we learned earlier, our lives are meant to be good and to run smoothly. If our circumstances seem chaotic or out of control, it is because we have somehow unbalanced them. One of our greatest challenges is to maintain balance in every aspect of our lives. This is not always an easy thing to do, and so this aspect of our spiritual growth can become an ongoing work in progress. We must strive to think calmly and rationally, to not allow our emotions—especially our fears—to overwhelm us, and to put all things into perspective.

One thing to remember about the Law of Balance as we study mediumship is this: being a medium is only one aspect of our lives. All of us must learn to work it into our daily practices without sacrificing the other important components of our existence. I started studying mediumship in 1997 when my twin boys were only a year old. I had to make some sacrifices on both ends of the spectrum in order to do so. I carved out time in my schedule to meditate, to go to classes, and even to go on weeklong seminars so that I could continue to grow spiritually. I also put on hold some interesting spiritual studies I would have liked to pursue so that I had ample time to spend with my babies and my husband. My family must always come first in my life. I made a vow to my husband, and by extension to my children, a long time ago that I have every intention of keeping. My life is a constant high-wire act. I'm always thinking many days ahead and trying to balance my work time, my play time, my family time, my study time, and my writing time, along with everything else that needs to get done. I'm sure that you will also have to modify your schedule if you truly wish to learn about mediumship and incorporate working with Spirit into your life. Just remember to keep it all balanced. Don't overdo studying and neglect another important area in your life. Believe me, those loved ones will keep you sane when nothing else will!

Natural Law #7: The Law of Use

The final law we will discuss here is a natural extension of all the laws that have come before it. The Law of Use tells us that energy cannot be destroyed. It can only be changed into something else, and scientific law supports this. Look at the three forms of water: solid (as in an ice cube), liquid (as we usually see it), and vapor (as in steam). The water has not been destroyed when we freeze it; it has simply taken another form.

This same principle can be applied to spiritual things. The ability to communicate with Spirit is a spiritual talent. In order to achieve this communication, we must work hard and train our minds to open to the process. Once we've achieved contact with Spirit, we must maintain that contact, and we must strive for even better communication. We have been entrusted by Creator to be responsible for our own abilities. If we don't hone our skills, we won't be able to rely upon them for very long. And if we know that we have these skills and that communication with Spirit is possible, why would we ignore this ability? Why wouldn't we do our very best to become adept at communication? This is what the Law of Use is all about. We must use our minds in a positive way in order to grow spiritually. This law doesn't just address mediumship. It encompasses all of our work in positive thinking and in creating a more abundant and loving life on this planet, as well as every other good action and thought that brings us closer to Creator. The Law of Use encourages us to be active participants in our spiritual growth.

Summing Up

By now, you hopefully have a better understanding of some of the underlying principles that govern mediumship, specifically in the form of the Natural Laws of the Universe that oversee every aspect of this world. We've discussed definitions that should help you to comprehend the remainder of the information in this book, and we've investigated the roots of modern mediumship by looking at the past. I would certainly encourage you to dig even deeper into any of these subjects that interest you. Knowledge is power; you can't go wrong by learning everything you can. And if you ask, Spirit will most definitely lead you to the sources that will help you in the best way possible.

In our next section, we will begin preparing ourselves for spirit communication by preparing our minds and bodies. As we move forward, you'll need to have a journal in which to record any experiences that you have. This journal can be as simple as a spiral notebook, or you can keep loose-leaf pages arranged in a binder. Whatever you feel most comfortable with is fine. Once you have this, take a deep breath, adjust your thinking cap, and follow me on to the next section.

Part 2

PREPARATION
of the
MIND AND BODY

So you're ready to begin working as a medium. What happens now? You just stand up and start giving messages from Spirit, right? Or you hang out a shingle that declares you "Jane Doe, Medium" and wait for the phone calls to come rolling in.

Oh, if only it were that easy!

One of the most frustrating things about being a medium is the process itself. I don't believe in pulling punches, so let me be honest with you right from the start: mediumship is work. It is not a walk in the park. It does not come easily to everyone, and to do this work and do it well, you must have dedication and perseverance. You have to be willing to spend time honing your mediumship skills. And above all, you have to want to be a medium for the right reasons.

So why do you want to be a medium? Turn to a fresh page in your journal and write down your answers to that question. I'll wait for you . . . take as much time as you need.

4 I Want to Be a Medium When I Grow Up

Finished? Great. Let's explore your answers for a few moments. There really are no right and wrong ones here. Some, however, are better than others, and I think you'll see why when we discuss this issue in more depth.

Not too many people utter these words as a child: "When I grow up, I want to be a medium!" I can't imagine what some adults might say if their son or daughter made this pronouncement. So why do we, as adults, come to this work and decide that we want to do it? What answer did you write on your paper?

I didn't start out as a medium. Actually, I had no idea what a medium was until I was in my late twenties. I did, however, become very interested in tarot cards when I was in high school. A good friend of mine bought a deck for herself, and when she showed them to me, I was so enthralled that I had to have a deck of my own. I started learning how to read tarot at sixteen, using a book to guide me. All through college, I did readings for friends. I even did a speech on tarot reading in one of my college classes. It was a fun hobby, and I was always pleased when someone I'd read for came back to me and said, "That reading you gave me was right on the money!" I would usually smile and shrug, saying, "Well, the cards are usually right." I never even considered the question of what might be influencing the cards to fall in a certain way.

I changed and grew over the next few years. As I got older, I started to explore more esoteric ideas, including alternative spiritual paths. I became very interested in Wicca, which encouraged the everyday practice of meditation. I started to understand the concept of energy and the way it influenced our bodies, minds, and spirits. Working with different energies in Wicca also opened me up to the concept of other entities in the astral world. When the opportunity to study mediumship in-depth with a teacher presented itself, I was more than ready. I'd been doing professional tarot readings for a few years by that time, and I wanted to bring even more accuracy and information to the clients who came to me for guidance.

For me, doing professional readings was a process that evolved. I didn't start reading tarot because I wanted to be a professional reader. That came much, much later. I enjoyed reading cards, and I enjoyed the time I spent with the people who came for readings. I liked answering their questions and helping them to sort through their problems. Reading for others made me feel as if I was helping them. My whole life, I'd been involved in service-oriented professions, and reading was just one more in that long line. Some people are naturally inclined toward service, and I was (and still am) one of those people.

This brings us back to the question "Why do you want to be a medium?" Truly, to be a good medium, you must want to help others and to be of service to humankind. No motivation should be stronger than this one. By opening yourself up as a conduit to Spirit, you are undertaking a huge responsibility—to the sitter who seeks out your services, to Spirit, and to yourself. People who ask you to read for them bring very real, very important situations and problems to you. They seek guidance and understanding, and they expect real, solid answers that they can rely upon. Spirit will provide these for them, make no mistake, but your relationship with Spirit must be a priority in your life to be able to access this information for them. Sincerity, honesty, and humility go a long way in cultivating a tight relationship with Spirit, and one thing that solidifies it is a true desire to serve others.

Another good reason to study mediumship is to grow in your own spiritual understanding. Learning about mediumship and how it works opens up a whole realm of realities that many people have never considered. In this book, some of these concepts will be introduced. This may be the first time you've run across this kind of thinking, so see how it feels to you. Does it make sense? Is it something that you can relate to or understand from your own experiences? I'm not here to convert anyone to my way of thinking; I can only give to you, the reader and explorer, the knowledge and the answers that I have discovered based upon my own experiences. You must draw your own conclusions and find your own truth. But if you have put your personal spiritual growth at the top of your priority list, studying mediumship can only help you. It will certainly not harm you in any way.

So what are some unacceptable reasons for studying mediumship? A need for attention is the first one that comes to mind. I have met people who attempt to do this work because they like the attention they get. These are the folks who tell everyone they can that they possess a "gift" for talking to Spirit, and then they bask in the limelight when their supporters ooh and aah over their talent.

Let me get one of my pet peeves out of the way here: the ability to communicate with Spirit is not a gift, at least not in the sense that some people have it and some people don't. Mediumship potential is present in *every person*. Granted, some individuals have an easier time establishing a connection with the spirit world and maintaining it. This doesn't mean, though, that these people are gifted! I can ride a bicycle; however, I've had three major accidents while doing so, at different times in my life. I still enjoy riding, but I am cautious when I do it, and I certainly don't brag that I'm the best rider in the world. Mediumship is the same: everyone can be taught how to connect, but not everyone is able (or willing!) to ride in the Tour de France. Some people need to work harder at their mediumship, whereas others breeze through the training. This is typical of many tasks in life; why should learning to connect with the spirit world be any different? Don't ever let any medium or psychic claim he is better than you. He may have worked very hard to get where he is, but that doesn't mean you can't get there, too.

Another shaky reason for wanting to become a medium is a desire for fame and fortune. Mediumship has become en vogue in the last few years, and there are several mediums who have gained celebrity because of this public fascination for the work. Most of these people deserve every bit of the attention they receive, because they are good at what they do and they have the best interests of their clients and audiences at heart when they are working. However, I feel very confident in saying that these famous mediums didn't start working with Spirit because they wanted to be celebrities or because they wanted to get rich quick. This should not be your motivation, either. As I stated before, mediumship is hard work. It is also work in which your clients are anticipating a reasonable (for the most part) amount of accuracy and truth. You won't last very long as a professional medium if you can't deliver the goods, just as an architect or an accountant won't be in business if she can't produce what she's promised her clients. It's fine to expect compensation for time and energy spent when you reach the professional level, but please don't let money be the motivating force behind anything that you do.

Now that we've discussed some of the reasons for studying mediumship, let's begin to prepare ourselves for the undertaking. It is important to concentrate on both our bodies and our minds as we attempt to reach the realm of Spirit.

5   The Five Senses

Most of us are aware that we possess five senses. These senses allow us to process information from the physical world. Sight, hearing, taste, smell, and touch all bring us different sensations that are processed through our brains and help us to understand what is happening around us. Small children learn many things by putting items in their mouths, by stretching out their fingers to grasp, and by seeing smiles or frowns on the faces of their caregivers. They learn very quickly what certain favorite foods taste like, how soft the fur on the cat is, and how clapping their hands makes Mommy laugh. When you stop to consider it, the way that we learn from our five senses is quite an amazing process.

Just as we use our five senses in our everyday life to connect with the physical world, we as mediums learn to use our spiritual senses to communicate with the spirit world. For each of the five physical senses that we possess, we also have a parallel spiritual sense. We'll discuss each one in turn.

Clairvoyance

The word *clairvoyance* comes from the French, meaning "clear seeing." Clairvoyance is the ability to see Spirit or to see images, pictures, and symbols that are sent from the spirit world. The young boy in the movie *The Sixth Sense* possesses extraordinary clairvoyant ability, as he is able to distinctly see the spirits who surround him. Of course, this is a Hollywood representation of mediumship, and they make it look much easier than it really is! Most clairvoyant mediums see within their minds rather than physically seeing the forms of people and other entities in Summerland. Clairvoyants also may be able to see auras, the energy fields surrounding the physical bodies of all living things.

Clairvoyance can also be an umbrella term used to gather all of the spiritual senses into one easy-to-remember word.

Clairaudience

Clairaudience means "clear hearing." A clairaudient medium hears voices and other sounds that come from the spiritual planes. These can be words, ambient sounds, proper names, or strings of sentences, depending on the medium. All of us are used to the normal sounds of everyday life, like a song playing on the radio or the hum of the computer monitor as we work at the office. Mediums (and sometimes others) can occasionally hear with their physical ears similar sounds or words produced by Spirit. There have been many documented instances of spirit voices captured on tape, having been recorded during séances, during readings, and even on people's telephone answering machines! This is simply more proof that Spirit exists all around us, whether we are aware of the presence or not. Clairaudience, though, is usually perceived as a distinct voice heard with inner ears or in the mind. It is different from the voice we hear in our heads on a regular basis, the one that tells us that we need to pick up the kids from school, that we must stop and buy milk on the way home, that we shouldn't be so critical of our sister's new boyfriend. Clairaudient messages are often hard to decipher, and it takes work to become adept at picking out the special voices that speak to us from Spirit.

Clairsentience

"Clear feeling" is the best definition for *clairsentience*. This spiritual sense is often called *impressional mediumship*, because it relies on the distinct feelings that the medium has when giving a message. Clairsentience often involves the medium being overcome by an unrelenting sense of what needs to be said, but the message does not come into the mind in any distinct way. It is more of a gut reaction, a clear and undeniable feeling that the medium has to speak about certain issues, give a particular name, or go to a specific person when giving messages to a large group. Clairsentience is a very common way for many mediums to work; if you asked them how they received their messages from Spirit, they wouldn't be able to define the process for you. It is more accurately a simple "knowing," without a clear understanding of how the medium came into possession of the actual information.

Clairaugustine

The spiritual sense of *clairaugustine* corresponds to the physical senses of both smell and taste. This sense is most often perceived in a physical way, through phenomena that may occur during a reading or séance. A medium, and the others gathered to communicate with Spirit, may clearly smell a scent in the room during the sitting. Pipe smoke, tobacco, perfume, and baking smells are common odors that come through. A medium may also receive a particular taste in her mouth while doing a reading, perhaps one associated with smoking cigarettes or a sourness associated with lemons. This is just another way for Spirit to communicate certain kinds of information to the medium, who can then pass this on to the sitter. Clairaugustine sensations often accompany one of the more common forms of mediumship, like clairvoyance, clairaudience, or clairsentience.

6   Discernment

One of the hardest tasks to learn when studying mediumship is *discernment*. As defined by *Webster's New World Dictionary*, to discern means "to perceive or recognize; make out clearly—to perceive or recognize the difference." This is absolutely what every medium must be able to do: to distinguish between her own thoughts and the messages that come from Spirit.

Sounds easy, doesn't it? Truthfully, however, this is the most challenging of all the skills a medium learns, because it takes a long time to develop discernment. It takes a commitment to Spirit that is enduring and focused. It also demands something from the mediumship student that is not always easy to give: trust.

The issues of trust and discernment bring us to the two most important rules in mediumship.

Rule #1: You Control Spirit

You have absolute control over everything that happens to you while working between the worlds. This whole Hollywood idea of demon possession and evil spirits? Don't you believe it for a second. As the medium, you and only you control which spirit beings make contact with you. Yes, there are negative energies that may try to connect with you; they may even try to attach themselves to your energy. Can you stop this from happening? Absolutely, without a doubt. We're going to talk about how to avoid this type of encounter in a moment. For now, realize that every spirit entity that exists will not have access to you, simply because you will control what touches in with your energy. Spirit can never make you do anything, say anything, or be anything that you don't want to do, say, or be. Creator has blessed us all with free will, which means we always have a choice and we can always control our actions. Just as we can hang up the telephone when we no longer wish to speak to an abusive caller, we can also refuse to have contact with a belligerent spirit from the Other Side.

If you remember nothing else about mediumship, this first rule is the one thing you should ingrain into your mind over anything else.

This brings us to the second rule of mediumship:

Rule #2: Give What You Get

Although the primary reasoning behind this rule is to give all the information brought to you by Spirit as honestly and objectively as possible, this rule has another side to it as well. The foundation of this rule is *trust*. Trust your instinct; trust what the little voice in your head is saying; trust what you're seeing in your mind. You're not making it up. What in the world do you have to gain from making up scenarios in your head? When you think about it logically, it makes no sense that you'd have all these visions, words, and feelings jumbling around in you, making you question everything you sense. In magickal training, there is a saying: "The belief in the magick is the magick itself." The same sentiment applies to mediumship work. You have to believe in the validity of what you're doing and in the truthfulness of the messages that you receive, or you will never be a successful medium. How can you become a successful anything when you doubt your ability all the time?

Discernment comes with time, but it is always important to *set your intention* when working with the spirit world. This is one of the primary factors in establishing contact with Spirit, and it is the best way to ensure that only the highest and the best information comes through when you are working. It is a main component of protection work, and every medium is responsible for protecting herself when working between the worlds. Remember the first rule of mediumship? Say it with me now: *You control Spirit.* How does a medium set her intention and protect herself from unwanted and negative entities? Through prayer and meditation.

Although meditation will be discussed further and in more detail later in this chapter, let's do an exercise together now. This is a very simple way to protect yourself. You can use this exercise every day as a way to rid yourself of unwanted negative energy and stress, as well as using it before attempting to touch in with the spirit world. Read through it first before you try it, and then, once you know what to do, go back and give it a whirl.

White Light Meditation

Sit in a comfortable chair with your back straight and your feet flat on the floor. Choose a place that's free of distractions (no telephone, television, noisy children or pets, and so forth) and close your eyes. Take several deep breaths in through your nose and out through your mouth, feeling your body begin to relax as you breathe. Bring your attention to the center of your body, to the point right above your navel. This is your solar plexus. Feel your attention telescope down to this tiny point in the center of your body. Say in your mind, "I am centered and balanced. All is well and safe."

Now bring your attention outside your body. As you watch, see all around you a beautiful, bright white light. This light shines down from above your head and encircles your whole body in the shape of an egg. It travels under your feet, over your head, and on both sides of your body, cocooning you in its warm radiance. You are completely surrounded and enveloped by this beautiful white light. This is the white light of love, the blessing of the Universe, of Creator, of the All, and it totally surrounds you now. Say to yourself, "I am safe and secure in the loving light of the Universe. Nothing but good can come to me, and nothing but good can come from me. I am safe."

Take a few moments to enjoy the beauty of this light. Then open your eyes, feeling safe, secure, and at peace.

How did you do? How do you feel right now, having just experienced this? Jot down your perceptions in your journal. If you don't feel like you could see the light, or if you feel that your visualization wasn't clear or sharp, don't worry about it. We all learn at different paces. For some folks, seeing pictures in their minds is hard work. Believe me, if you truly want to work in the spirit world, you'll become more and more adept at meditation, because you'll need to practice it regularly to keep yourself in tune with spirit energies.

Now, getting back to discernment: if you set your intention, that you are only working from a place of love and for the highest good, you should be confident that all of the messages you receive while working with Spirit are accurate and reliable. That makes spirit work sound really easy, and in essence, it should be. The problems start when we, as human beings, get in the way. Our egos try to take over, and our doubtful minds, the scientific and skeptical sides of our natures, begin to tear down our faith in ourselves and in Spirit. The more we work, however, the more we come to trust Spirit and the more faith we have in ourselves. It is a process. Be gentle with yourself as you go through it.

7 Physical versus Spiritual Awareness

Developing physical awareness will help you to become a better medium. This idea sometimes seems strange to new students, because really, how physical can mediumship work actually be? It's not like lifting heavy boxes or running a marathon, right?

Or is it?

As mentioned earlier, each phase of mediumship, each spiritual sense, also corresponds to a physical sense. When you are more in tune with your physical senses of sight, hearing, touch, taste, and smell, the subtle changes that Spirit may use to send you a message will be much easier to receive.

Try this: when you're out taking a walk somewhere, look around you. *Really look* and *really see* what's going on. Many of us are so busy that when we stride through the mall or the grocery store we don't really notice anything that's happening around us. Next time you go out, focus your mind to notice *everything*. Really look at the people who pass you on the street. What color are their clothes, their hair? Can you smell anything in the morning air? Coffee? Pastries? The trash from the overflowing can? Do you hear the misfire of a vehicle starting, the grind of a nearby garbage truck, the hum of an air conditioner? Can you taste the crispness of approaching autumn on the wind, or the salt water from the beach two blocks away? Observe and note these occurrences. Marvel at it all. Our world is truly a remarkable place.

Once you've taken more time to notice the physical energies around you, you will most likely find it easier to experience the spiritual energies surrounding you as well. When you've really focused your eyes on seeing the physical, you might suddenly see a flash of light or color out of the corner of your eye. There wasn't anyone or anything within ten feet of you, so what was it? More than likely, you just saw a spirit entity pass by. They move so quickly and at such a high energy vibration that they are often seen as no more than flashes, blurs of light and color, or wavy lines. When you see these, though, know that you are seeing Spirit! The more you work, the clearer these passing energies will become to you.

You'll also notice that your inner, clairaudient ear becomes more sensitive when you make an effort to listen harder to the sounds around you. Take some time and really listen to a piece of music. Put on headphones if you can. Extract from the piece each instrument in turn, and follow what that particular drum or guitar is doing. When someone is speaking to you, put down your pencil or stop folding the laundry and actively *listen* to him. Is his voice strained with tension? Is he out of breath for some reason? These can be important clues about his emotional state or the circumstances around him, which can in turn help you to understand him better. Soon, as your physical ears become more sensitive, your inner, clairaudient ear will pick up whispers of names, words, or even whole sentences. It will be easier to distinguish the voice of Spirit from the endless chatter of your own mind if you already know what the latter sounds like. Listen and see what Spirit has to tell you.

In your everyday life, remember to take stock of how you're feeling. Do you find yourself physically tired at your boring job? Are you more energized when you go outside for lunch? Why do you think this is? Could it be that the actual energies of these environments are affecting you? When you can recognize how you feel physically at certain times and in certain places and situations, it becomes easier to understand when the energies change. As you continue to study spirit communication, you may begin to notice that the energies around you change when spirits gather close to you. Perhaps you feel a tingling sensation in your body, or maybe you literally get goose bumps when there isn't a significant temperature change. These are just some examples of what may happen when your inner clairsentience begins to kick in. Note these feelings, because they are signs of how your mediumship is progressing.

Communicating and living with Spirit employs all of our senses. You may find that one sense more than another is heightened for you. This is perfectly normal. I tend to be mostly clairaudient and clairsentient when I work with Spirit. I will hear names, snatches of phrases, singing, and other sounds. I will also feel compelled to say something very specific to my reading client, knowing that I can't go on in the reading until I impart that information. I have often wondered if this is because I've had very poor eyesight since my childhood. I think my other senses, especially my sense of hearing and my sense of touch, have heightened over the years to compensate in some way. I don't tend to see much clairvoyantly, but even this is changing as I evolve as a medium. After all, everything is possible with God. You will change, too. Remember, without change there can be no growth. And each person's growth progresses in the correct and best manner. Keep noting these little shifts in perception and you'll be well on your way to working more closely with Spirit.

So is mediumship physical work? It can certainly feel like it sometimes, even when you're just sitting in an office and advising clients in thirty-minute sessions all day long. Along with my work as a medium, I'm also a licensed massage therapist. I can honestly say I've been more exhausted after doing six readings than after the same number of hour-long massage sessions, where I'm actually pushing, kneading, and otherwise physically manipulating a client's body. Why is this?

Spirit communication relies on the Law of Vibration (see Part One, "Starting from Scratch"). Remember that this law states that everything in the Universe vibrates at a different rate of energy. In order to communicate with the spirit world, we as mediums must *speed up* our energy vibration, and Spirit must *slow down* its vibration. Thus, we meet somewhere in the middle in order to give and receive messages. This heightening of our energy vibration to connect with Spirit can be very taxing to the physical body. One important step in mediumship training is learning to maintain our physical and energetic bodies. Let's look at this energy system now, so that we can understand how it relates to mediumship.

8   Auras and Chakras

In her excellent book *Hands of Light: A Guide to Healing through the Human Energy Field,* Barbara Ann Brennan defines for us what she calls the Human Energy Field: "It can be described as a luminous body that surrounds and interpenetrates the physical body, emits its own characteristic radiation and is usually called the aura" (1987, 41).

Every living thing has an aura. In famous paintings of Jesus, the saints, angels, and other enlightened beings, a halo of golden or white light appears around the heads of these figures, symbolizing, of course, their ascended states of consciousness. In esoteric thinking, however, it is believed that the artists were trying to represent visually the dynamic and pervasive aura of the master they depicted.

People talk about the ability to see auras, and I am often asked in classes or in readings if I can see auras. I can, but it is not the primary focus of my work. I have to work harder to actually see the person's aura. It's easier for me to tune in and ask the spirit guides and teachers around the client if there is anything about her energy field that I should mention. However, you may discover that you are adept at seeing auras and other components of the energy system. More than likely, this will happen if you tend to be more clairvoyant

47

in your work. Take a few moments to try these simple exercises, and record any impressions that you have about them in your journal.

To See Auras

Have a friend or pet sit on a chair in front of a white wall. If you don't have someone to ask or a pet to bribe (my pets never cooperated in these exercises when I wanted to practice!), position a large houseplant in front of the wall. (Remember, plants are living things too and will emit an aura.) Turn the lights in the room down low and sit across from your subject. If you wear glasses, take them off. Stare at your subject with "soft" eyes. Look at it but don't drill your gaze into it. Don't try to catch its eye. Let your mind wander a bit; this will help to "soften" your gaze as you look at your subject. In a few moments, you should become aware of a band of light about six inches or so from your subject's body, usually concentrated around the head and shoulders or the top of the plant. This is the aura. Its thickness may vary, and you may even be able to perceive certain colors. It may look rather yellowish on one side, with a splash of dark green over the head and a streak of pink on the right side. You may also notice sparkling or shimmering in the energy field. These are just examples of colors and patterns you may notice. Jot down what you see. Congratulations! You've just seen your first aura!

To Feel Auras

Again, enlist your friend or pet for help in this exercise. Have your helper sit in a chair or lie down so that he is comfortable. A plant may also be used and positioned in a chair so you can reach it. Standing behind your subject, rub your palms together briskly and then hold them about an inch apart. Can you feel the heat, the tingling, or any other sensations between your hands? This is energy that you are feeling. Now take your hands and gently lower them until they are about six inches from your subject's head or from the top of your plant. You will feel a change in your palms when you hit the subject's aura. Do you feel heat or vibration or cold in your hands? Even a slight change is what you're seeking here. You've found the energy field! Congratulations! Make notes of your observations in your journal.

If you do any further research and study into the fascinating field of energy work, you'll find that the aura is actually made up of a complex layering system. We're not going to discuss any of that here, but if this information piques your interest, please refer to Ms. Brennan's book. It's probably one of the best on the subject.

Another important component of the body's energy system are energy centers called *chakras*. Taken from Sanskrit, the word *chakra* means "wheel." In the human body, there are seven major chakras, or wheel-shaped energy centers, and there are twenty-one minor ones. We're only going to discuss the major chakras here, and only briefly at that. For more information, you might read a book like *Wheels of Life: A User's Guide to the Chakra System* by Anodea Judith, Ph.D.

The seven major chakras begin in the lower body at the base of the spine and progress up the backbone. Lest you think the chakras can only be accessed from a posterior position, imagine them instead as round beams of light that radiate to the front of the body as well as to the back. Each chakra emanates a specific color, and each controls a variety of physical, emotional, and spiritual health issues. On the next page is a chart listing each of the seven major chakras in order, as well as their correspondences.

As you can see, the chakras in the energy system affect each person on every level possible. When our chakras are balanced and clear of negative blocks, we feel terrific. When our chakras are clogged up in some way, or unbalanced, we may notice challenges that manifest in our emotional, mental, spiritual, or physical states.

CHAKRA	LOCATION	COLOR	CENTER OF . . .	CONTROLS . . .	HEALTH	IN BALANCE	UNBALANCED
1. Root	Base of spine	Red	Survival	Life force	Weight issues	Feel secure and stable	Feel fearful and anxious
2. Navel	Beneath navel	Orange	Self-gratification	Vitality	Abdomen, hips, genitals, lower back	Feel healthy pleasure	Emotional problems, over-attachment
3. Solar Plexus	Above navel	Yellow	Power	Clairsentience, gut feeling	Digestion, diabetes, chronic fatigue, organ disorders	Acceptance of ourselves and others	Anger, domination, aggression
4. Heart	Center of chest	Green	Love	Activation of higher chakras	Heart, circulation, breasts, arms, lungs	Feel confidence, compassion	Feelings of loss, grief, sadness
5. Throat	Center of throat	Blue	Communication	Clairaudience	Throat, thyroid, neck, jaw	Feel clear, unobstructed in expression	Fear of expression
6. Third Eye	Center of forehead	Indigo	Intuition	Clairvoyance	Eyesight, memory, head, sinuses	Insightful, intuitive, psychic	Poor vision, headaches, bad dreams
7. Crown	Top of head	Violet	Consciousness	Cognition	Migraines, tumors, amnesia	Spiritual balance, connection to Creator	Confusion, apathy, skepticism

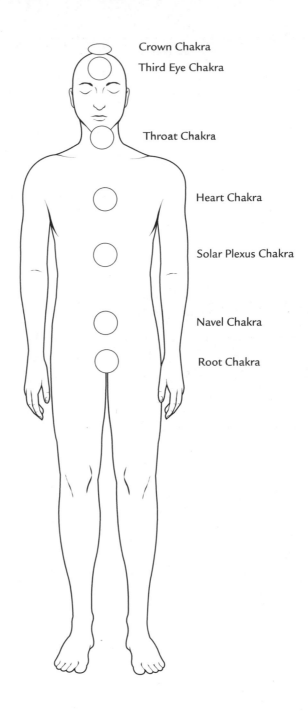

Crown Chakra

Third Eye Chakra

Throat Chakra

Heart Chakra

Solar Plexus Chakra

Navel Chakra

Root Chakra

The Energy System in Readings

Knowledge of the aura and the chakras helps us as mediums in several different ways. First, if you are clairvoyant, you may actually see a blockage in a client's energy field. Often, these types of problems appear to our clairvoyant eyes as dark spots, hazy areas, or blotches. If you are clairsentient and are close enough to the client, the energy field or certain areas of it may display distinct drops or increases in temperature or vibration where problems are manifesting. The ability to sense these challenges and point them out to a client in a reading can be most helpful in their quest for spiritual, emotional, mental, or physical healing. One word of caution, however: remember always that you are not a medical professional. You can get into a mess of legal complications if, in a reading, you dispense anything that can be interpreted as medical advice. We'll discuss this more in depth in Part Five, "Readings and Sittings." For now, just realize that any knowledge you have of the energy system may help you to give a more accurate and meaningful reading to a client.

Using the chart provided, take a moment now to go through the following quiz. See what answers you can come up with and write them in your journal.

Chakra Interpretation Quiz

1. You notice in a female reading client that her solar plexus chakra emits a sickly pale yellow color. How could you interpret this?

2. A male client you are reading for appears to have a long, spiky beam of dark energy hitting his crown chakra. You feel this is a physical manifestation in his body. What would you say to him?

3. A lady who comes for a reading seems to emit a rich, bluish purple energy directly in the center of her forehead. What would you tell her about this?

4. A female reading client's chest area is covered in a gray mist when you look at her. How could you interpret this?

5. A man who sits with you for a reading emits a violent red energy from his root chakra. What kinds of issues could this man be facing?

Did you come up with some answers? Let's go through them together.

For the first question, about the lady with the sickly yellow solar plexus energy, did you think this problem might be connected to her personal power? You certainly could have interpreted this to be a physical challenge involving her digestion or one of the other listed health concerns, but every physical problem usually has an underlying root issue that is causing it. In cases involving the solar plexus chakra, the issues of personal power are often prevalent. If this were my client, I would interpret this to mean that the woman feels out of control in her own life or that she feels controlled by other people or forces. She needs to claim her personal power and be confident in herself and her decisions. If other people are the issue, she needs to stand up for herself. She needs to be assertive (remember, there is a difference between being assertive and being aggressive) and uncompromising when expressing her needs. Personal power issues are at the heart of solar plexus problems.

In our second example, the man with the crown chakra spike, what did you say? Did you interpret this to be a migraine? I would if he were my client, especially if I felt this to be a physical challenge that needed to be addressed. In energy work, you can often see a migraine or its aftereffects in the aura as a spike. It could also mean the man is heading for a migraine soon if he doesn't watch his diet or his stress level. I would ask my client if he has a history of migraines and make my recommendations from there.

What did you think about the woman with the bluish purple light in her third eye chakra? If this were my client, I would be very excited about seeing this, because this kind of energy is a clear sign that the woman is very psychic. This woman is on (or should be on) a spiritual path, and Spirit is trying to work very closely with her. She is intuitive and open, and she needs to trust her feelings, for they'll usually be right on the money.

How did you interpret the gray mist appearing in the chest area of our fourth client? This affects the heart chakra, which is the center of love, and this would be the key issue underlying any problem in this area. Is this woman in a bad relationship? Has she just experienced a loss in her life? In a reading setting, you may receive more information about the actual circumstances from Spirit, but the bottom line is that this woman needs to love herself. Heightening her self-esteem and remembering that she is deeply loved by Creator will help to clear out this gray energy and allow the green light of the heart chakra to shine forth.

How about our last client, the gentleman with the extremely red root chakra energy? Remember that the root chakra is connected to survival; an out-of-balance one can represent fear and anxiety. Perhaps this man is upset over losing his job or is afraid his source of income is about to disappear. On a basic level, these are survival issues, and this is how they may manifest in the body. If I saw this in a reading, I would start by counseling the client about his career.

How did you do? If you came up with different answers from these, that's OK, but do look back at the chart to see if you understand how I arrived at my answers. Of course, in any reading setting, there are really no absolutes. You must interpret things as best you can and as Spirit guides you. However, Spirit can only use the information that is in your mind to try to send messages. If you have a good idea of how to interpret the chakras and their colors, you have one more tool for Spirit to use to communicate.

The Medium's Energy System

An understanding of auras and chakras also helps us as mediums to take better care of ourselves. Remember when I said that readings could wipe you out physically? Are you beginning to see why this may happen? For a better understanding, let's look again at our imaginary reading clients.

Let's say that client number four comes in for a reading. You notice immediately when she walks into your office that she is lethargic when she moves. Her speech is monotone; her face, void of expression. You see the gray mist shrouding her heart chakra and realize that she has recently suffered a loss. She confirms that her husband has left her for another woman and that she came for a reading to find out if he will ever come back to her. Wow. Heavy stuff to begin with, is it not? You proceed to spend forty-five minutes talking to her about self-esteem issues, and you help her to understand that she must first love herself before she can hope to have fulfillment in her other love relationships. You know, however, that this is not really what she wanted to hear in the reading, and she leaves with the gray mist still congealed around her chest. After she's gone, you notice that you now feel heavy, groggy, and pessimistic. What happened?

More than likely, you have absorbed some of your client's negative energy into your own aura. This probably happened because you didn't take the time before your reading to center yourself and to do a protective meditation. Because of the nature of energy and the way it moves, it is very easy for it to blend with other auric fields and to stay trapped there until cleared away. It can also accumulate in certain spaces, especially in rooms used for healing or counseling, which is why it's a good idea to do some energetic house cleaning every now and then. This is a major reason that many mediums feel worn out after only a couple of readings. If you find yourself absorbing unwanted energies from clients or just other people in your life, protecting yourself and clearing space are two things you can do to help. I'll admit it: I'm guilty of not taking care of my energy body the way that I should. I've been told time and again by Spirit that if I'd do my protective meditations more often, I wouldn't feel so tired. But I'm human, and I make mistakes. Don't we all?

We'll discuss in a bit some other meditations you can do to help balance your energies and to keep you in good shape, physically and energetically. Before we talk about meditation, however, we need to first talk about another physical process in the body. It is one that is vital to our existence, but one we take for granted and don't even notice most of the time. Let's talk about *breathing*.

9   Breathing

We inhale, we exhale—one cycle of breath. Pretty simple, isn't it? Maybe so, but do you realize that many people don't breathe correctly? Sounds questionable, doesn't it, considering all of us are walking around, alive and kicking, and we must be breathing in order to do that. Breathing, however, is an important component for preparing to work with Spirit, so we'd better investigate and make sure we get it right!

All of us breathe, true enough. But most of us breathe shallowly or only in our chests. Do you realize that the normal lung capacity of a person is 6 liters but during normal respiration only 450 to 500 milliliters are inhaled or exhaled? That's a big difference. But why should this matter to us as mediums?

Breath ties the body to the mind. Slow, deep breathing helps the body to relax. Our minds also slow; our thought processes wind down. The endless, everyday chatter of our brains quiets and recedes, allowing us to drift peacefully into another state of consciousness. This type of breathing, the deep, slow breathing that involves not just the chest and lungs but the diaphragm as well, is what we as mediums want to achieve. Deep breathing helps us to enter a meditative state more effectively, which is vital to mediumship work. Let's try something right now.

Deep-Breathing Exercise

Sit with your feet flat on the floor and your spine straight against the back of the chair. Be sure to sit up nice and tall—no slouching or hunching over. Place the palm of one hand on your belly, right over your navel. Now take a normal breath. Did your hand move? If you're like most people, you may have felt a slight rise and fall as you breathed, but nothing much. This is because, like most of us, your breathing is taking place mostly in your chest.

Keep your hand on your belly. Now *slowly* inhale through your nose to the count of eight. Count it in your head as you breathe in: *one—two—three—four—five—six—seven—eight*. Did your hand move this time? It most likely did, because by slowing your breathing and forcing yourself to inhale to the count of eight, you made your diaphragm engage. Your diaphragm is a big sheet of muscle that forms the bottom of the thoracic cavity in your body, and it helps to push air in and out of your lungs. As you inhale, your diaphragm drops, making the space bigger. As you exhale, the diaphragm rises, helping to expel any air that needs to leave the body.

Now let's take our exercise another step further. Again, keeping your hand on your belly, inhale to the slow count of eight. When you get to eight, hold your breath for a count of six. Then, exhale your breath *slowly*, through your *mouth,* to the count of ten. That's it: *one—two—three—four—five—six—seven—eight*—keep pushing!— *nine*—almost there!—*ten*. Whew! Was that harder than you expected? Most people leave a lot of residual air in their lungs when they breathe, which becomes stale. Imagine how much better your body would function with fresh air all the time. Your mind is no exception. Deep breathing helps to nourish and revitalize the entire body while allowing it to relax. This is just what we need to be doing to begin our study of meditation.

10   Meditation

A lot of information has been written on the science and practice of meditation. In teaching meditation over the years, it's been my experience that many people don't really understand what they are supposed to be accomplishing through meditation. Many people also become easily frustrated with the process, which causes them to give up. I don't want you to be one of those people, so let's try to demystify the meditative process enough so that you can reap its many rewards.

There are many reasons to meditate. In our society today, with all the noise, speed, and stress, there is a need for quiet, peace, and relaxation. Remember that the Universe is all about balance. You can't have light without dark, male without female, positive without negative. The same is true of activity, whether it be in your mind or in your body. To balance activity, there must also be stillness. This is where meditation comes in.

The primary purpose of meditation is deep relaxation. From this relaxation we can achieve stress relief, inner calm, and a sense of profound peace. This peace can lead us into releasing anger, grief, fear, or other negative emotions that hold us back spiritually. As we progress in our meditations, we may find solutions to problems, more creativity in our lives and work, access to physical and emotional healing, and the ability to contact higher powers. All of these wonderful scenarios can be ours if we can master this skill called meditation.

Regular meditation practice is an essential part of mediumship development. I suggest to my students that they try to meditate once a day. To be successful, you need to be diligent about this. Remember, you're making a commitment here to your own spiritual growth and enlightenment. Meditating for ten or fifteen minutes a day is not asking a lot, even though time is usually precious to most of us. We are all busy. (I live in the real world, too, you know.) I guarantee, however, that if you give yourself this quiet time to center and balance in meditation, these fifteen minutes will make the other sixteen waking hours of your day more peaceful, more productive, and more balanced in every way.

So how shall we get started? Try to make your meditation time the same each day so that it will become a habit. Are you a morning person? Maybe it would suit you to meditate before you drink your coffee, while the house is still quiet. If you tend to be a night owl, perhaps the best time for you is in the late hours, before you go to sleep. If you're a stay-at-home mom, maybe you can squeeze in your meditation time while the baby is napping or while Junior is watching *Toy Story* for the hundredth time. (Hey, I have twin boys, so I know what it's like!) You may have to try different times before you come up with the best scenario for you. Keep experimenting, and ask Spirit to help you find the ideal practice. Assistance is always just a plea away.

A few other tips for successful meditation: Find a spot where you won't be disturbed. Take the phone off the hook and shut the door so you won't be interrupted. Turn the lights down low. Burn a candle and/or incense if that helps you to relax. Try to meditate sitting up, with your feet flat on the floor and your arms and spine comfortable, as we did in the earlier breathing exercise. If you lie down, you are signaling your body to sleep, and that's probably what will happen. If you do fall asleep, don't worry too much about it. Your body obviously needs rest. If you find yourself falling asleep often when you're trying to meditate, switch your meditation time to earlier in the day, perhaps shortly after you get up in the morning. Eventually, you'll understand what works best for you, and you'll look forward to your meditation time.

Don't become frustrated if nothing much happens the first few times you meditate. If you have never done this before, give yourself time to get acclimated to this new practice. I have found that people often get frustrated because they aren't "instantly enlightened" the first time they meditate. People, I've been meditating regularly since I was about twenty-one, and I'm *still* not enlightened! I anticipate meditating until the day I die, and I still won't be enlightened then, either! It's a *process,* which means that every person will go at his own pace. Remember when I said becoming a medium wasn't easy? Establishing a meditation routine is just the beginning.

Over the next few pages, I'll introduce you to some different guided meditations. These are designed to help you relax and to open up your consciousness on an energetic and spiritual level. Read through the meditations first before you try them to get an idea of what you need to do in each one. Some may seem very simple. They *are* simple, so that you can really practice visualizing and experiencing everything that the meditation script suggests. Take your time with each meditation. With each script, I have included a suggestion of how long to practice this particular meditation before moving on to the next one. Consider taking these time periods to heart. The more you practice, the better medium you'll become. You may find that you like particular meditations better than others. Once you are meditating on a regular basis, you can certainly pick and choose which exercises you want to practice. For now, try to go in order, and be sure to take time after your meditations to record any impressions that you have in your journal.

Some people like to take the transcripts for the meditations, read them aloud into a tape recorder, and play them back over headphones as they meditate. This is a perfectly acceptable practice, especially if you are having trouble concentrating during your meditations. Or, if you can find someone to work with, you can have him read the meditation aloud to you as you relax. Whatever works best for you is the right choice.

Simple Relaxation Meditation
(*Every day for one full week—ten to fifteen minutes*)

Get comfortable in your meditation chair. Close your eyes and become aware of your breathing. Consciously begin to slow your breathing, deepening your inhalations and concentrating on pushing out every bit of air you can as you exhale. Breathe in through your nose to the count of eight, hold the breath for six counts, and then exhale that breath, slowly and evenly through your mouth, to the count of ten. Continue breathing like this for at least three cycles.

Now, as you continue to breathe, bring your awareness to your feet. Feel your feet as they rest on the floor. Allow your feet to feel heavy. In your mind, tell your feet to relax, and notice how all the muscles in your feet seem to soften as you suggest this. Tell yourself, "My feet are relaxed."

Bring your attention up your legs. Feel your legs under you, supporting you in the chair. Allow your legs to become heavy; allow all the muscles in your legs to relax and soften. Tell yourself, "My legs are relaxed."

Now move your attention up to your hips, your pelvis, and your stomach. Feel these areas begin to soften. Allow your belly to relax and push out. Tell all the muscles in your hips to lengthen and relax. Tell yourself, "My hips and abdomen are relaxed."

Bring your attention up your body to your torso. Suggest to your chest that it relax, and feel the weight in it lift and lighten. Feel all the muscles in your torso soften and lengthen. Tell yourself, "My torso is relaxed."

Now move your attention to your fingers and hands. Feel them become heavier as the muscles seem to melt. Let all the tension in your hands drain out, and feel them soften. Tell yourself, "My fingers and hands are relaxed."

Allow your attention to settle on your arms and shoulders. Feel your shoulders drop as you suggest relaxation to them. Notice all the tension draining out of your arms as the muscles soften and lengthen. Tell yourself, "My arms and shoulders are relaxed."

Bring your attention to your neck. Allow all of the tension in your neck to drain away, and feel your neck muscles relax and soften. Tell yourself, "My neck is relaxed."

Move your attention to your face and head. Allow the muscles in your face to relax. Feel your jaw drop open as the tension there is released. Feel yourself soften as you tell yourself, "My face and head are relaxed."

Now enjoy this relaxed and peaceful feeling for a few moments. Note how different your body feels and remember this.

(Take five minutes of quiet reflection.)

Now it is time to awaken your physical body. Know as you do, however, that your physical body is now relaxed and revitalized and that you will carry this peaceful feeling with you for the rest of the day.

When you feel ready, open your eyes. Move slowly and deliberately as you come back into your physical self.

Simple Protection Meditation
(*Every day for one full week—ten to fifteen minutes*)

Begin by closing your eyes and getting comfortable in your chair. Concentrate on slowing your breathing, bringing yourself into a cycle of deep breathing as in previous meditations.

Bring your attention to your feet. Notice any dark areas, any gray or black spots, in your feet. This is tension that is trapped in your body. Allow this darkness, this tension, in your feet to drain out of your body. See the stress draining away. The darkness moves out of your feet and drains into the earth, dissipating and transmuting into valuable energy. Tell yourself, "My feet are relaxed."

Move your attention up to your legs. Watch all tension and stress in your legs drain down from your hips, down through your knees, down through your ankles, out through your feet, and into the earth. Tell yourself, "My legs are relaxed."

Next, bring your attention to your torso. See any negativity and stress begin to drain out of your torso, starting in your chest, draining down into your abdomen, moving down into your pelvis, down through your legs, out of your feet, and into the earth. You are releasing all of this dark stress and tension from your whole torso, and it all drains out of you. Tell yourself, "My torso is relaxed."

Move your attention to your fingers and hands. Allow them to relax, and allow any tension or negative energy to drain out of them through the tips of your fingers and out into the ethers. Your hands become heavy as all this energy drains away. Tell yourself, "My fingers and hands are relaxed."

Now your attention moves up your arms to include your limbs and your shoulders. Allow any tension or stress in your arms to drain away. All the heavy negativity drains down from your shoulders, through your arms, into your hands, and out through your fingertips. Tell yourself, "My shoulders and arms are relaxed."

Move your attention up to your neck and head. Allow any stress or tension in these areas to drain away. It moves down from the top of the head, draining through the neck and into the shoulders, moving down the arms, through the hands, out of the fingertips, and into the ethers. Tell yourself, "My neck and head are relaxed."

Now see your whole body as if looking at it from outside of it. See that it is relaxed and at peace.

Above your head, you now notice a beautiful, bright white light. This is the Universal Light of Love, Divine Energy, and it pulsates right above your head, above the crown chakra at the top of your head. See your crown chakra open as if it's a flower, and watch as this beautiful, bright white light of the Universe pours into your crown chakra. It begins to fill you as water fills an empty cup, filling your feet, filling your legs, filling your torso, filling your hands, filling your arms, filling your neck, and at last filling your head.

As it fills you, your body becomes like a beacon, shining as bright as the light itself. As you watch, see the bright love light spill over from your crown chakra as your entire body is filled, cascading down around you like a magnificent waterfall. This light totally surrounds you, totally penetrates you, and you are filled and encompassed by the loving light of Divine Creator. You are protected and loved beyond measure, and your heart and soul are filled with a sense of profound peace and safety.

Take a few moments to enjoy this beautiful energy, this great gift from Creator.

(Pause and enjoy for five to ten minutes.)

And now it is time to come back to the physical world. Know as you come back, however, that you will still be completely filled with the loving light of Creator and that you will carry this love and light to every person you touch in everything you do. You remain enveloped in Creator's divine love and protection, and you are relaxed and at peace as you slowly gain awareness of your surroundings. Open your eyes slowly and move deliberately. Be gentle and easy with yourself as you come back into your physical body.

Chakra-Cleansing Meditation
(*Every day for one full week—ten to fifteen minutes*)

Begin by sitting comfortably in your chair, closing your eyes, and starting to breathe deeply. Do your deep breathing for several cycles, feeling your body relaxing with each breath. With each exhalation, more tension and stress leave your body, and with each inhalation, positive energy and relaxation enter your body.

Now bring your attention to the base of your spine in your body, and see there the circular orb of energy that is the root chakra. It is red in color. Look at the chakra closely and notice any dark areas, any patches of negativity that you see. As you watch, allow these dark patches to clear away; let the negative energy drain out of the root chakra, leaving only a beautiful, vibrant ruby red color. When all the darkness has been cleared from the chakra, watch as it begins to spin, slowly at first, then to a nice, steady rhythm. As it spins, the chakra begins to open, unfurling its petals like a flower in the sun. It shines with its beautiful red light, and you know this chakra is clear and balanced.

Move your attention up your torso to the navel chakra, which is located directly under the navel. This energy center is orange in color. As you look, notice any dark areas of this chakra that need to be cleaned. Allow this dark energy to drain out of the chakra, leaving only bright, beautiful, vibrant orange. Watch as this chakra begins to open and spin, blossoming and shining with the prettiest orange color you've ever seen. You know that your navel chakra is balanced and clear.

Now allow your attention to travel up to your solar plexus chakra. It is located above the navel, in the center of your abdomen, and this energy center is yellow in color. Notice any dark patches in the yellow, and allow this dark energy to begin to drain out of the chakra. All of the negative energy trapped in the solar plexus chakra drains away, and the chakra begins to spin with a beautiful, vibrant yellow color as bright as daybreak. You know that your solar plexus chakra is clear and balanced.

Watch as your attention moves up to your heart chakra, located in the center of your chest. This energy center is green in color, but you notice any areas that seem marred by dark patches. Allow that negative energy to drain out of the heart chakra, until it brightens and pulsates its breathtaking kelly green color. The chakra begins to spin as you watch, and you know that your heart chakra is balanced and clear.

Now your attention moves to your throat chakra, in the middle of your neck. This energy center is blue in color. Notice any dark areas in this energy center, and allow those to begin to fade away. The chakra begins to spin, a bright blue beacon of light, and you know that your throat chakra is clear and balanced.

Next bring your attention to the center of your forehead, to the third eye chakra. As you watch, any dark, negative energy shading this chakra begins to drain away, and the chakra starts to spin, revealing its true, deep blue-purple color. The indigo of the chakra is strong and vibrant, and you know that your third eye chakra is clear and balanced.

Now move your attention up to the top of your head, in the center. Here you will find the crown chakra, which is violet in color. As you watch, allow any dark energy to drain out of the crown chakra. The crown chakra begins to spin, casting its clear violet light as it unfurls on your head. You know that your crown chakra is balanced and clear.

Bring your attention back out so that you can observe your entire body. See all of the cleared chakras spinning and casting their colorful lights around them as you watch. Note the feelings you are having as you realize that all of your chakras, your energy centers, are cleared and balanced.

Now it is time to come back into your physical body. Take your time, and begin to feel the chair underneath you, the floor beneath your feet, your hands, and so on. When you feel as if you are truly back in your physical body, slowly open your eyes.

The next few meditations are designed to help you hone your visualization and concentration skills. In the first meditation, you will be visualizing a ball. The object of the meditation is to concentrate on really seeing the ball and to keep focused on it for the entire meditation. If you find your attention beginning to wander or the picture in your mind beginning to fade, bring your focus, both mentally and visually, back to the ball. As you practice this meditation, increase the time you spend doing this. Start out with only five minutes, and increase it to ten over the course of your week.

Concentration Meditation #1: The Ball
(*Every day for one full week—five minutes to start,
increase daily to a total of ten minutes*)

Begin by closing your eyes and getting comfortable in your chair. Breathe in through your nose, hold, and exhale through your mouth for at least three rounds. Feel relaxation begin in your body. Allow all of your body to become heavier and more relaxed with each breath.

Now see in your mind's eye a ball. It can be any type of ball you desire. What size is the ball? Is it small, medium-sized, or large? What color is it? Is it textured or smooth? Simply see the ball from all angles, and keep your mind focused on the ball. Continue to bring your attention back to the ball any time your mind starts to wander.

Concentration Meditation #2: Many Balls
(*Every day for one full week—ten minutes*)

Sit in your chair comfortably and close your eyes. Begin deep breathing for at least three cycles, allowing your body to become relaxed and heavy.

Now see in your mind your favorite ball. See it sharply and well-defined. Notice the color of the ball, the texture of it, the size of it.

Now your ball begins to change. It becomes a basketball. If it was already a basketball, it does not change and continues to be a basketball. See the bright orange of the ball. Notice the knobby texture of the ball and how big it is.

Again your ball begins to change. It moves from being a basketball to being a golf ball. See how small it becomes, and see the indentations all over the surface of the ball. Notice its white color.

The ball begins to change again. The golf ball grows into a baseball. See how much larger it becomes. Notice how the surface of the ball becomes smooth. See the stitches in red that embroider the white background.

Now, again, the ball changes. It becomes a beach ball. It grows larger, and the smooth surface changes color, divided into several different hues.

At last, the ball changes back to your original ball. Allow this ball to fade away as you begin to come back into regular consciousness. When you open your eyes, you're wide awake and relaxed.

Concentration Meditation #3: Word Meditation
(*Every day for one full week—ten minutes*)

Begin by sitting comfortably in your chair, closing your eyes, and breathing deeply to relax your body. Perform at least three rounds of deep breaths before beginning.

Keep your mind free of distractions as you begin to concentrate on one word. It can be any word you like, such as *love, peace, God,* or something else with a positive connotation. Any time your mind begins to wander, bring it back to your word. Keep saying the word to yourself over and over in your mind. Find a rhythm that you like and repeat the word in your mind. Continue to do this, and feel what emotions and vibrations this particular word brings to you.

The next meditation is one you will use many times in the weeks to come. It is the basic meditation we will use as we begin to work more with those in the spirit world. It might help you in this meditation to read the script into a tape recorder and play it back over headphones as you do the meditation. If you have someone to work with, you can have him read the script aloud to you as you meditate. Again, whatever works best is right for you, but try to really enjoy this meditation. You'll become more and more familiar with it as you practice it, and it will become a haven for you.

Special Place Meditation
(*Every day for one full week—fifteen minutes at least*)

Begin by getting comfortable and closing your eyes. Take a deep breath in through your nose, hold it for three seconds, and then release it slowly through your mouth. Take another deep breath, hold, and release. Continue with this type of deep breathing, and as you inhale, imagine bringing positive energy into your body along with the oxygen of the air. See white light moving into your body through your breath. As you exhale, imagine that you are releasing through your breath any tension, any stress, any negative thoughts or emotions you might be holding. See these leaving your body as a stream of gray as you let your breath go. Continue to breathe deeply, visualizing yourself becoming more relaxed, more at peace, and more positive and happy with every breath you take. Imagine the white light energy filling up your entire body, from the tips of your toes to the top of your head, until you shine as brightly as the sun.

Once your body is completely filled with this beautiful, bright white light, imagine that light spilling out of the top of your head and cascading down, all around your body. It envelops your whole body, forming a protective shell all around you—to your sides, underneath your feet, above your head. It fills in all the space until you are completely surrounded by this beautiful, bright white light. Notice how safe, how at peace, you feel within this light. This is the white light of the Universe, the loving energy of the All, the great Creator, that surrounds you and protects you. Know that you are safe within this light and that everything that comes to you and goes from you is positive and good.

Now, in your mind's eye, see before you a path that leads into a lush wood. Look above you and notice the blue sky, the warm breeze that caresses the trees around you, and the fragrant grass that waves on either side of the path. You see that the path leads into the forest, and although you cannot yet see where the path goes, your curiosity gets the better of you, and you begin to walk. As you walk, you enjoy your surroundings, feeling relaxed and at peace as you move along.

After a moment, you see that the path you follow leads straight to a very special place. Maybe it's a beautiful meadow filled with flowers. Perhaps it leads to a white, sandy beach, where the ocean waves lap the shoreline. Maybe you find a moss-covered cottage that you can enter and explore. Or maybe your path ends in a lush garden, filled with fountains and benches and every type of foliage imaginable. Wherever your path leads, this is your special, sacred place. It is a place of your own creation, and it can be anything you want it to be. It can be indoors or outside, warm or cool, natural or synthetic: it is yours and yours alone. This space will become your haven, the place where you will spend your meditation time, so be sure to make it as special and as beautiful as you yourself are. Take some time now to look around, to add to the surroundings, knowing that all you need to do is think of something you would like and it will appear in your special space. Enjoy your time here.

(Take five to fifteen minutes of quiet time to spend in this new space.)

Now it is time to return to the physical world. As you prepare to leave your sacred space, realize and know for certain that you can return to your special place anytime you wish. It will always be available to you, always ready to welcome you and help you to feel safe and relaxed.

And now, as we count backward from three to one, you are starting to come back to this time and space—*three*. You are beginning to feel your fingers and your toes—*two*. You are becoming aware of the room around you. And as we say the number one, you are wide awake and at peace, wide awake and relaxed.

A Few More Words about Meditation

Meditation is a practice that is vital to becoming a good medium. One of the best things meditation does for us is nurture in us a sense of peace and well-being. It also helps us to touch in with our own divinity and thus builds a bridge for us to touch the divine energy that is all around us. Having this connection to Creator is of utmost importance. No matter what anyone may tell you, mediumship is important and sacred work. Communicating with Spirit and serving humanity as a medium is a calling, much like becoming a doctor or a minister. Once you have heard the calling to serve in this way, it won't go away, no matter how much you try to deny it or ignore it. Living with Spirit can be exciting and exasperating, often at the same time. Feeling grounded, centered, and balanced is imperative as your world begins to open up to these possibilities and as you explore the huge impact you yourself have on the Universe and your little corner of it. Meditation helps you to achieve this sense of peace that is so needed.

We're moving forward now in our study of mediumship, but you must remember never to neglect your meditation practice. Continue working with these meditations every day as you read the next sections, because they will help you to prepare to meet your own spirit guides and to begin to work with them.

Summary

You've done a lot of work in this chapter, whether you realize it or not. Take a moment to flip back through your journal. If you've been recording everything I've suggested, you should have several pages filled with notes by now. This is a record for you of your spiritual journey, and you should be proud of the steps you've taken already. You've learned about the spiritual senses that correspond to our physical ones and how a medium uses these in her work. You've seen how important paying attention in the "real" world is and how it helps us to see more clearly the messages that Spirit may send from the Other Side. You have a better understanding of the energy system of the body and of its components, the aura and the chakras, and you've learned how maintaining these helps in mediumship development as well as physical, emotional, and mental well-being. Deep, cleansing breathing has become a new practice for you, especially when you are meditating, and you are starting to see the benefits of what a regular meditation routine brings to you. Great work so far!

Now we're ready to continue on in our studies. The next section is an exciting one, and you will use many of the skills you've learned in this chapter as we begin our study of spirit guides. Are you ready to meet yours?

Part 3

WHO'S WHO
in the
SPIRIT WORLD

Each of us has many friends in the spirit world. They are available to us at all times. They help us to cope with any situation or problem. They inspire us, listen to us, assist in our decisions, and make us laugh: their attributes are as varied as they themselves are. Cultivating a relationship with these spirit friends can enhance our lives more than we can possibly imagine. Learning to communicate with our spirit guides and teachers is a long, sometimes frustrating process, but the rewards of diligence, patience, and commitment are truly worth the efforts.

In the following pages, you'll find descriptions of our *inner band guides*, which are the guides who are closest to you. You'll also be introduced to the concepts of *Ascended Master guides, angels,* and *outer band guides.* After each section, there are meditations listed that you may use to contact each of the entities discussed.

Meditation is a vital component of spirit communication. Everyday meditative practice is something I encourage with all my students. Once you get to know your spirit teachers, you must maintain that relationship, just as you maintain friendships with the people you know here on the physical plane. You e-mail and telephone your friends to catch up with them and their lives, don't you? The same can be said of our relationships with those in Spirit: the more we cultivate our connection to them, the stronger our bonds become. Meditation is one of the best ways to keep in touch with our spirit friends.

There are many ways to meditate. We've already discussed several techniques for relaxation and consciousness expansion. In this chapter, we will build on those earlier exercises, and I will give you sample guided meditations that you can use to open up the lines of communication between you and Spirit. Remember that you can read these transcripts into a tape recorder if you want and play them over headphones while you work, if that will help you to concentrate. You'll find the way to work that best suits you.

Remember, don't give up if you don't instantly connect with your guides. I'm sure it took some time with the earlier meditations before you felt comfortable and satisfied with the results. You are undertaking a learning process, and so are your spirit people. They are trying hard to communicate with you, just as you are attempting to communicate with them. Sometimes, though, we have to learn a different language to understand each other. In music, for instance, a student must learn the names of symbols and notes. He must incorporate into his own vocabulary new words and meanings so that he can communicate with his teacher and with other musicians. As in any discipline, we must be patient as we learn to recognize our guides and their messages. I promise you: if you stick with it, you will see results. You will get to know your guides, and you'll start to see their influence in your life.

Now let's meet some of our wonderful spirit friends. We'll begin, as we usually do in a relationship, with an introduction to each one.

11   Joy Guides

You know that friend of yours whom everyone loves, even your grumpy old Uncle Herb? You know the friend I mean: she's always the life of the party. She can make even the most sober occasion cheerful, and she always knows just the right thing to say at just the right moment. Her laugh is contagious; her smile lights up a room. She never seems to run out of energy, and she's ready at a moment's notice to go shopping, go bike riding, or do whatever fun activity you have planned. Nothing seems to dampen her buoyant spirit. She exudes warmth from every pore of her being, and if she wasn't so darn loveable, you'd probably get aggravated with her plucky *joie de vivre*.

This indispensable friend has a counterpart in the spirit world. All of us are blessed to have a *joy guide* as one of our closest spirit companions. As their titles indicate, joy guides have been entrusted by Creator to remind us of the lighter side of life. They help us to feel good about ourselves and to boost our self-esteem, and they aid us in making decisions in our lives that will bring us happiness. They are usually our closest spirit friends and confidants, and they want nothing more than to see us rejoice as we journey along our spiritual path.

Because they so easily honor the happiness that Creator intends for our world, many joy guides appear to us as children or young adults. Young people have not yet forgotten how to have fun, and the reality of living fully in bliss radiates from them like a beacon. Joy guides can be male or female, and they usually range in age from five to fifteen, give or take a few years. Joy guides often wear bright, colorful outfits, and they enjoy anything with vibrant energy. Flowers, glitter, merry music, dancing—all of these things delight joy guides and help to call their energies to us. Many joy guides even have silly names to further remind us of the power of laughter and the high vibration that it brings. A close friend of mine, the male pastor of my church, has an adorable joy guide named Tinkerbell. One member of my congregation has a joy guide named Bubbles, and, believe me, her energy perfectly matches her name. While studying at Camp Chesterfield one seminary week, I attended classes and services with a tough Italian guy from Chicago. Turned out he had a joy guide named Twinkle Toes, and when she came through with a message in chapel one evening, no one was more thrilled to hear from her than her cool, aloof counterpart. Spirit really does know just the best way to make us all laugh!

I consider my beautiful joy guide, Mara, to be one of my dearest friends. We have been working together for a very long time, and I think we know each other quite well. Over the years, I have learned many personal things about her. Her favorite song is "You Are My Sunshine," and every time I stand up to give spirit messages in front of a large group of people, we sing it for her. I often sing her song while I'm puttering around the house or driving in my car, just to honor her. Just hearing her song brings her energy closer to mine, and I am immediately infused with her loving warmth. Mara appears to be about fourteen or fifteen, and she has long, wavy dark hair that falls to her waist. I have never seen her without a smile on her face, whether it be a calm one of reassurance and hope or a huge grin of mischievousness. She often wears green or blue, and she enjoys sunflowers. My husband, who doesn't share this affection for flowers, understands that I am honoring Mara when I hang pictures of them around our house.

Your joy guide will have favorite things, too, and once you meet her and begin to work together, you might consider utilizing these preferences to bring her energy closer to you. If you don't already have a sacred space where you perform daily rituals or prayers, try to find a little niche where you can begin to practice your meditations and exercises to get in touch with your guides. Use a nearby shelf on the wall, or a small table in the corner, to display items that honor your guides. Try to choose a favorite room in your home, one where you feel secure and happy. I usually meditate in my bedroom, propped up with pillows against the headboard of my bed. My altar space is across from the bed, on top of the standing jewelry armoire my husband gave to me as a wedding present. It is decorated with many things, including candles, incense burners, statues of deities, photos of special people, crystals and stones, and tokens that honor my guides. I often change things around on my altar as I find something else that reminds me of Spirit's presence in my life. Right now, on one corner, there is a candy wrapper tucked under a large quartz crystal. The story of how that candy wrapper came to me is interesting, and it demonstrates how our spirit guides can make their presences known to us.

Some friends of mine hold a meditation circle on Wednesday evenings. I am not always able to attend, but I try to go once a month if I can work it into my schedule. One night, we experienced great success at bringing in many Ascended Master guides (energies like Jesus, Mother Mary, and Kuan Yin) to speak to us. It was an exhilarating circle, and as we were getting ready to go home, we were all chatting excitedly about everything that had happened. The hostess of the circle carried around a dish of wrapped chocolate candies as we bustled about, and I took one even though I try not to eat sweets late in the evening. My energy was so high, I was hoping to help ground myself by indulging. As I unwrapped my candy,

I mentioned to another lady that it was interesting that Mara, my joy guide, hadn't come through to speak that evening. I laughingly suggested that maybe she felt intimidated by the Ascended Masters' energies and decided not to participate. I popped the chocolate into my mouth and started to crumple the foil wrapper up for the trash can, but something inside the wrapper caught my eye. I smoothed it out and realized there were little messages printed on the inside of the foil for each candy. What did my message say? "You are my sunshine."

Thank you, Mara, for that gentle and loving reminder that you are always with me.

Your joy guide is ready and willing to touch you in his or her own special way. Once you open up the lines of communication with yours, your life will never be the same.

12   Protector Guides

What do you imagine when you hear the word *protector*? Do you think of police officers, firefighters, or soldiers? Maybe your mind turns instantly to the Secret Service agents who secure the president, or maybe you think of someone closer to home, like the bouncer at your local watering hole. Perhaps you envision someone tall, with broad shoulders, a beefy build, and an imposing presence.

If these are the images that come to mind, you are well on your way to understanding the role of a protector guide. Each of us has been given a spiritual bodyguard. Our protectors have been entrusted with our safekeeping as we walk our path through this physical incarnation, and most of us truly give them a run for their money as they attempt to keep up with our many adventures.

Like joy guides, most protectors have lived a physical life at one time or another in history. Many protectors come from indigenous cultures that were close to their land and its defense, like the Native American peoples in North America. Some protectors have a background in military tactics and war. Often, protectors are skilled warriors, and they continue to emanate these protective energies as they do their jobs in the spirit world.

You may ask, "Why would I need a soldier or a Native American brave protecting me? I'm just a _____ [housewife, computer programmer, landscaper—fill in your own occupation]." You may think such protection is unnecessary. This is simply not the case, no matter how mundane or ordinary our lives may seem to be. We all face potential dangers every day, and these are the situations our protectors help us to overcome.

For instance, how many of us drive? Most parents do; in fact, many spend large parts of their days in minivans and SUVs, transporting their charges to and from various activities. So let's imagine for a moment that you, Mom or Dad, are driving a car full of kids home from their late soccer game. Darkness has already fallen, and you have to drop all of the children off at their various homesteads. It begins to rain, hard, and the windows of the car fog up as the temperature outside falls. The kids are rowdy from the excitement of their game, and you try to stay focused on the slick road ahead of you while refereeing a fight in the backseat between two teammates. You grip the steering wheel harder; your heart rate elevates; you feel the beginnings of a tension headache creep up the back of your neck. Suddenly, the wheels of the car hydroplane as you plow through a particularly large puddle, and the car begins to slide . . .

Sound familiar? Well, hopefully, you've never been this close to an accident. But this scenario, with the team of rambunctious kids and the tension connected to carpooling, is probably one to which a lot of people can relate. It's an everyday situation. And all of these people, from the soccer mom to the goalie in the backseat, are in danger here. This is where our protector guides come into play.

Whenever I find myself driving through lousy weather conditions, or whenever my kids (including their friends or not) are especially distracting on a road trip, I always call in my protector guide, Arthur, and ask for extra protection as I travel. I ask him to surround the car with protective energy and to help me to stay extra alert. I also entreat him to help us reach our destination safely. That's really the whole point, isn't it? I haven't had one accident since I started asking for my protector's help in these types of situations, thank God.

It's also a good idea to call on our protectors whenever we feel vulnerable, especially in a potentially dangerous situation. Suppose your car breaks down and you need to walk to the nearest gas station to call for help. What if it's late at night and the road isn't especially well lit? This is an important time to enlist your protector guide and to allow her to do her job.

Of course, common sense is something that we all need to employ. We cannot replace it by relying solely on our spirit helpers. The Universe responds best to our requests when we act accordingly, and our guides, who serve Natural Law, are no different. They cannot interfere in any situation if we haven't first asked for their assistance. That would be a violation of our free will, and they will not do that. But we have to remember to stay out of harm's way, too, just as much as we have to remember to call on our guides when we need them.

As a theatre major in college, I kept very late nights, often spending my evening hours in the theatre rehearsing or running a show. I lived on campus all four years of my college career, and I would walk home from one side of campus to the other to reach my apartment. It was usually very late, very dark, and very lonely on these nighttime excursions.

I recall stage-managing a show my junior year with a female director, Pat, who was much older than me. She had returned to school to get her bachelor's degree after working in the "real world," and she was in her forties. After finishing up one evening, Pat asked if she could give me a ride home. I laughed and told her my apartment was on campus and I was used to walking. Pat was absolutely horrified and gave me a serious lecture on the dangers of a young, pretty (bless her!) college co-ed walking unaccompanied late at night across a deserted campus. She insisted on driving me back. I countered by saying, "But I've never had any problems before." Pat answered firmly that I must have some really big angels watching out for me, but she wasn't taking any chances and neither should I.

My wise, older friend was absolutely right. As a mother in my thirties, I shudder to think of my carelessness. What was I thinking? Thank God for Arthur, my protector. I like to think he was doing the best job he could at the time, even though I had no idea that he even existed. Maybe he even prompted Pat to speak to me that night. She changed my way of thinking, that's for sure.

Our protector guides also help us in repelling and dissipating negative energy. Remember, everything in the Universe is made up of energy. There are energies all around us, everywhere we go. Have you ever walked into a room and immediately felt uncomfortable? You are picking up subconsciously on the negative energy present in the space. Have you ever met someone and immediately felt drawn to him or her? Again, you are sensing the other person's energy and finding it compatible with your own. Some of us are more sensitive to energies than others, but we all are susceptible to attracting and holding on to different energies. These energies, be they positive or negative, can become attached in our auras, the energy bodies that surround our physical bodies. Sometimes, we become overwhelmed by these negative vibrations, and they begin to affect us physically or mentally. Often, if we are not in tune with ourselves, we cannot figure out why we feel tired, angry, or upset.

We are all exposed to different energies throughout our days. Think about your place of employment for a moment. Is it brightly lit? Do your coworkers chat amiably with each other? Is there a feeling of comradeship and cooperation between the members of the staff? Do people from outside the workplace comment on how nice it is to visit? On the other hand, do you dread going to work every day? Why? Is it because your coworkers complain constantly about their jobs or their personal lives? Are there conflicts between staff members? Do you feel lethargic and empty when you are at work?

All of these are signals of the types of energies permeating your work environment. If you are usually happy at work, feeling productive and getting along with coworkers, then you are experiencing positive energies throughout your day, and your own aura will benefit from this. If you are frustrated at work, feeling angry and resentful of others, then you are being bombarded with negative energies. Your aura, your vital energy body, is picking up and carrying around these negative vibrations, causing you to feel emotionally and physically drained. And think about this: most of us spend forty hours or more at our jobs every week. Multiply that by fifty weeks or so, and the number of hours exposed to this type of energy per year is staggering. But short of quitting, what can you do?

Your protector guide to the rescue! Protectors are experts at dissipating negative energy in your environment. By calling for your protector's help, you can start to feel better in any situation, just by asking that he keep harmful and negative people and energies away from you. I can personally attest to how well this works.

Several years ago, I signed up at a local Renaissance festival to do clairvoyant tarot readings. I had been reading for years by this time, working at many psychic fairs and conducting parties for friends. I was very confident in my reading skills by this time, and I had begun to expand into mediumship readings, as I was studying hard and learning more and more about the spirit world with each passing day. I was excited by the prospect of meeting so many new people, working in such a fun, festive environment (I love Renaissance festivals as a general rule), and serving Spirit in such a productive way.

Unfortunately, not all went as I had envisioned it. The festival didn't have nearly the attendance it had enjoyed in past years, so there were many stretches of time when I wasn't busy. This was especially hard because my children were very small at the time, and the guilt about being away from them both days every weekend for eight weeks didn't make me very happy (or popular at home, for that matter!). The biggest disappointment to me, however, was the attitude of many of the fair patrons. A lot of people came up and literally laughed in my face when I explained that I was a spiritual reader. Many wanted a short "free reading," just to ensure that I was "good" and they weren't "wasting their money." (Just for the record, I did no free readings for these people.) Still others would come in, sit down for a reading, and play the game I refer to as "Test the Psychic." This occurs when no matter how many accurate details you give a sitter in a session, that person focuses only on the things that you *didn't* know. And of course, at a festival where alcohol was served, I had my share of drunks who staggered in. They could barely even focus their eyes on me as I talked to them, let alone comprehend the messages that came through from their spirit people.

One of my teachers at Camp Chesterfield would often echo a well-known biblical passage in our classes: "Don't cast your pearls before swine." I had no real understanding of what this meant until I worked those first few weeks at the Renaissance festival. And please, don't misunderstand my meaning: the folks who came to the festival were not terrible people. For the most part, they were simply men and women who had no real interest in spiritual understanding, and they were looking to be entertained. Working with Spirit and channeling higher messages from the other realms, however, is not meant to be entertainment. This was obviously a lesson Spirit wanted me to learn and learn well. By the end of the third weekend, I was frustrated and upset. I dreaded the upcoming five weeks, wondering if there was any way I could get out of my contract early without losing all the money I'd paid for my space at the fair.

One night, as I was meditating, it occurred to me to speak to my guides about the situation. My protector, Arthur, appeared. I said, "Listen, I can't keep doing readings in these conditions. None of the people who are coming care about what Spirit has to say. What am I doing wrong?"

He looked at me with such compassion and love, and he said, "Dearest one, you have neglected to ask for our aid."

I protested immediately. "That's not true," I retorted. "I always ask for your help when I read for people. I ask that the highest and best messages come through and that I render them in a way that the sitter can understand."

Arthur smiled gently. "Yes, you do. But you have forgotten to protect yourself. You are picking up negative energies that these people bring with them to your table."

I was exasperated. I knew he was getting at something, but he wouldn't come right out and tell me what to do. (Spirit is like that, people. You have to to figure it out for yourself.) "So I need to do more protective meditations?"

"Your meditation is adequate. It's the people who are coming to you, isn't it?"

The proverbial light bulb began to flicker in my brain. "Ohhhh . . . I need to ask that only the *right* people, people I can help with Spirit's guidance, come to me for readings. Right?"

Arthur smiled again. "I can only do what I'm asked to do, dearest. I can keep the negative people away from you. You've just never bothered to give me that task."

That weekend, as I was preparing to work, I made sure to ask Arthur to be present and to bring to me only people who needed my guidance and who would appreciate and respect my help. After that, I had no more negative experiences with the fair patrons. All of the readings that I did, although fewer in number, were well received. Now, whenever I work in a group environment, whether it's readings at a fair, clairvoyant circles, or messages in church, I ask Arthur to keep negative people away from me and to allow through only spirits who can touch in with people who appreciate their presence and assistance.

You might be thinking, "Well, is that really fair? What if those people truly need to be helped?" This is a valid point. I try very hard in my work to touch as many as I can, and I try not to screen out people whom I perceive to be problematic. The key word in that last sentence is *I*. I might judge a potential client to be someone I don't want to work with, but Spirit may see that person as integral to my own learning process as a spiritual being. I trust that my spirit guides and teachers are going to help bring me the lessons I need to learn and that those lessons will manifest in whatever forms I need. Yes, some clients are difficult. Sometimes, they are difficult because we need to set up our own boundaries and learn how to say no. Over the years, I have been taught this lesson time and time again. Apparently, it's one of the hardest ones for me to learn, because I still occasionally have to be reminded of it. But asking Spirit to surround you with people who support and help your energy is perfectly acceptable. When you are ready to have your limits tested, Spirit will also be more than happy to help with that task.

You too can reap the benefits of mental, physical, and spiritual protection. Your protector is awaiting your call. She can't do anything without your permission, so what are you waiting for?

13   Doctor Teachers

During my junior and senior years in high school, I had a very special teacher. Mr. G taught both of my advanced-placement English classes, and he introduced me to a vast, exciting world, one that exploded to life through the power of the written word. I studied Shakespeare, poetry, mythology, and world literature with him, and I savored my moments in his classroom, because his lessons were like no others. He made the stories of Hamlet, Odysseus, the Hunger Artist, and Holden Caulfield tangible and important to a group of seventeen-year-old girls who usually only cared about finding a prom date and fantasizing about some big-haired MTV god (it was the eighties, after all). Mr. G inspired me so much that I chose to go to college as a theatre education major. I too wanted to bring stories to life for kids in a classroom. My life didn't exactly end up the way I expected, but I never forgot Mr. G, and the love of literature that he stoked in me still burns brightly to this day.

I'm sure many of us have a favorite teacher from school, one who always comes to mind when we take the time to look back on those younger days. Probably the one quality that all of these favorite teachers possessed, the trait that makes them shine brightly in our shadowy memories, is that they inspired us to achieve our very best in their classrooms. In my case, Mr. G was a tough teacher. He expected excellence out of his students. The one time I didn't do my homework in English class and he caught me without it, I felt a shame more acute than with any other instructor before him. Why? Because I'd let him down. He expected better of me, and I blew it. Of course, he forgave these shortcomings, but he made me want to do better, to achieve more, to reach the highest potential I possibly could.

The same can be said of our doctor teacher spirit guides. Our doctor teachers are a huge asset to us because they are very concerned with our spiritual development. They are both our strictest taskmasters and our biggest cheerleaders as we grow spiritually. We can come to them with our spiritual questions, and they will try their best to help us find the answers we need.

Doctor teachers, also called doctors of philosophy, lived a physical incarnation at some point in history. Although they are called "doctors," this title is an honorary one bestowed upon them after a great deal of study in the spirit world. This title does not mean that they were medical doctors during their last physical incarnation, although they certainly could have been members of that esteemed profession. Only your own doctor teacher can tell you what he used to do here on earth. For instance, my doctor teacher, Dr. William Wilkins, was not involved in any way, shape, or form in the medical profession in his last lifetime. He was a businessman and devout Spiritualist from the late nineteenth century, so he is happy to help me with matters that revolve around Spiritualism and incorporating those beliefs into my life. He has his work cut out for him, too, because I have a very diverse spiritual and religious background and one of my chief missions in life is to incorporate all of these beliefs into a cohesive whole for myself. I feel Dr. Wilkins's presence most strongly when I am teaching mediumship development or when I am writing sermons and lecture materials for church, classes, and workshops. I know he's helping me as I write this, too. In fact, he has asked me to do something I rarely do, which is channel spirit energy as inspirational writing. Dr. Wilkins wishes to speak directly to you all, so I will allow him to do so here. (Note: Any references Dr. Wilkins makes to "the instrument" are references to me, the author. This is an old-time Spiritualist way for guides to talk about the people they are working with in the physical realm.)

It is my great pleasure to be given the opportunity to speak directly to you today from the world of Spirit. My name is William Wilkins, and I am the doctor teacher of the instrument whose words and thoughts you have been reading. We are most proud of our instrument for taking on this project, as it is one of vital importance to all humanity. We are also proud of each of you for following your instinct, the God-voice inside of you, that urged you to pick up this work. If you are reading this book, you are a lightworker, and your path is set to travel throughout your physical incarnation to bring light to others. You may think your work insignificant in the grand scheme of things, but nothing could be further from the truth. Each and every one of you has a significant contribution to make in the evolution of your world and in the elevation of spiritual understanding. Great and small, all works are important, so go about your daily tasks with pride in accomplishment, knowing that your intent to serve God keeps your vibration high and your mind on the true spiritual path to God.

A word about doctor teachers: we are here at your service. We know you have questions about your purpose and path in life. We know you seek knowledge and control over your lives, and this is right and good. God wants you to feel comfortable and confident in all that you do. He challenges you to constantly move forward, and to move forward with compassion, humility, and grace. You must remember and understand how special and loved you are by God and by all of your spirit teachers and friends. Your doctor teachers want to help you find your way in the world. It is sometimes a difficult path, and we are here to aid you just as much as we can. We are only a thought away; simply think of us, and we are with you. Tell us your needs, and we will strive to bring to you the situations and resources you need to achieve balance in your lives. We love nothing more than debating and discussing spiritual issues, so allow us to give you our views . . . but always remember, the choice never lies with us. You have all the power to change your lives and to fulfill your destiny as spiritual beings. We wish to help, and we constantly send you our love and regard.

As you can see from Dr. Wilkins's words, doctor teachers have a wealth of knowledge to share with us. They try to open our minds to spiritual possibilities and to lead us in the right direction for our best spiritual growth. Doctor teachers surround us with people and situations that will enhance our spiritual journey. For instance, have you ever gone into the bookstore and wandered around the New Age or self-help section, not really knowing why you're there? Next thing you know, the finger that you're tracing aimlessly along the spines on the bookshelf stops on one in particular. You pull it out, open it up, and are amazed by the information you find printed there. It's the answer to that nagging question that's been plaguing you for weeks! Next time, thank your doctor teacher for bringing you the information that you so desperately needed.

Your doctor teacher is waiting for you to call. Once you get to know this important spirit guide better, you will begin to recognize the signs of his presence in your life.

14   Doctor Chemists

Alchemy, as defined by *Webster's New World Dictionary*, is "a method or power of transmutation, especially the seemingly miraculous change of a thing into something better." An al*chemist*, then, is someone who is able to produce such a change. Interesting that we have a close spirit guide whom we call our doctor *chemist*, isn't it? Have you deduced from this definition with what area our doctor chemist guides might concern themselves?

If you guessed something to do with manipulating energies, you are close to the mark. Our doctor chemist guides have a couple of important functions, and both of them center around working closely with our energy bodies to bring about changes.

Doctor chemists are very concerned with our physical state and well-being. They are interested in us maintaining a healthy lifestyle, so they monitor our food and drink intake and can help us make good choices about diet. Closely linked with nutrition is exercise, of course, so our chemists can also help us to find and maintain an exercise regimen that is best suited to our needs. In addition to our day-to-day health, our doctor chemists can aid us in healing physical ailments that manifest in our lives. Of course, as in the case of protectors, it is always better if we work in accordance with our chemists to try to avoid potential problems before they arise. For instance, if you have lingering back pain, perhaps your chemist can help you find a good chiropractor or massage therapist instead of you waiting until your pain is so bad that you need to have surgery to correct the issue. Chemists are especially adept at helping you to find the solutions in the physical world that you need to address any conditions that your body may be manifesting. Tuning in and allowing yourself to trust this guidance is vital to utilizing the skills of your doctor chemist.

However, because our chemists are skilled metaphysicians, we can look to them to help manipulate the energy bodies surrounding our physical bodies to produce changes for the better in our physical selves. Energy healing works because the healer addresses the issue within the auric field of her client rather than working directly on the body itself. Many times, physical problems can be avoided by eliminating them in the aura before they manifest in the body. Our chemists can also help facilitate healing from their position in the spirit world. We need only ask for this assistance, and they will begin to work to bring the healing that we require.

As a healer myself, I never forget to ask my chemist to help in healing sessions I facilitate with my clients. However, we sometimes forget to ask our guides for aid in our own healing processes. It is difficult for me to remember to ask Black Hawk, my chemist, for healing when I have a headache or when my muscles are sore and aching from an especially long workout or a tough massage session. This is an area I need to work on in my own development, as Black Hawk has told me more than once, bless him. He gets his share of work, though, because I always call him in when my family is suffering, as the following story illustrates.

Not too long ago, my son Max came home from school with a headache. I had picked the boys up that day, and Max seemed especially lethargic when he got into the van. When I asked him about his day, he said he'd had a headache since lunchtime. When we got home, I gave him a snack, hoping that might help him, but half an hour later he was lying on the couch in tears. I sat down and cradled his head against my chest, and I was alarmed to feel what many energy workers call a "migraine spike" coming out of the left side of his head. I put my hand over it and asked him if his head hurt in that area, and he affirmed that it did. I was very upset. My husband and I have both suffered from migraines for many years, and one of my biggest fears in becoming a parent had always been that we would somehow pass this tendency down to our children. Anyone who has been debilitated by a migraine knows the incredible pain and anguish one can cause. The thought of my young son battling such agony, and the realization that he might have to endure bouts of them for many years to come, was torture for me.

But I wasn't willing to just give up. I told Max to close his eyes and that I would call in his doctor chemist to help us get rid of his headache. Although I know a couple of my sons' guides, I am not familiar with them all yet, and Max's doctor chemist was one I had not met. To facilitate the healing, I called to my chemist, Black Hawk, who is a Native American shaman and medicine man. I could literally feel Black Hawk's arms, in his winglike robe of feathers, come up around my own arms as I held Max against me. In my mind, I asked Black Hawk to bring in Max's doctor chemist, and I asked him to work with Max's chemist to help heal my son of this migraine. I held this thought in my mind as I sat with him, breathing slowly and steadily so that Max would relax. After fifteen minutes of constant prayer, I opened my eyes to see that Max had fallen asleep. I laid him down gently so as not to wake him and tiptoed out of the living room. When his dad came home from work an hour later, Max awoke, feeling refreshed and displaying his usual good humor and high energy level. I still don't know the name of Max's doctor chemist, but I trust that he and Black Hawk worked hard together to bring Max the healing that he needed.

Our doctor chemists can also work with us in an area that is important to those who serve humanity as mediums for the spirit world. Not all of us need this kind of help, so I will only touch briefly on it here. Some mediums are *physical phenomena mediums,* which means that through them, Spirit can produce physical manifestations and proof of its existence. When Spiritualism was popular as a "parlor religion" in the early part of the twentieth century, there were many mediums who produced a substance called *ectoplasm* in their séance rooms. This substance, which is grainy or cloudy to see, could form materializations of spirit people who wished to make their presences known to the sitters in the séance. It could also transfigure the face of the medium in a séance, causing the medium's appearance to take on the look of someone in Spirit. Ectoplasm could also pour out of the medium's orifices and be manipulated by Spirit to lift objects, such as the metal trumpets that spirit people used to magnify their voices. There were many genuine occurrences of ectoplasm, as well as many fraudulent mediums who used things like cheesecloth to mimic the appearance of real ectoplasm in the séance room. I don't wish to debate here the validity of physical phenomena. I can say, though, that I have seen ectoplasm for myself in séance rooms where I could detect no hint of fraudulent behavior, and I certainly believe it can be produced by the body and utilized by Spirit to prove its presence.

The production of ectoplasm is overseen by the doctor chemists we have working with us. If you are not a medium, then you needn't worry about this phase of work with Spirit. If you aspire to become one, it is an aspect of mediumship that you may or may not embrace after time. I think it is important to point out that at this time in history there are not many physical mediums demonstrating spiritual gifts. I have been told by my spirit teachers that this has something to do with the poor food supply that we ingest nowadays. Back in the heyday of Modern Spiritualism, many people still ate homegrown vegetables, eggs, meat, and other foods. They did not feast on junk food as we do, nor did their foods contain the alarmingly high amounts of preservatives and artificial ingredients that many of our foods do today. My spirit teachers tell me that it was much easier for the doctor chemists to manipulate the energies of those mediums, which is why physical phenomena was much more prevalent than it is today. Now, it is incredibly difficult for mediums to purge their bodies of these unnecessary and unhealthy dietary additives, which prevent much of the alchemy needed to change the physical body into a vessel for ectoplasm production. It is not impossible, I have been told, but Spirit has decided it is much more important to focus on the messages being conveyed at this time rather than the "fancy tricks" that used to shock and awe audiences.

Whether you are a medium or are just interested in getting to know your spirit guides, your doctor chemist is an important member of your band. The healing presence of your chemist will be one that you cherish once you get to know her better.

Meditation Work—Joy Guide, Protector, Doctor Teacher, and Chemist

Now that you've been introduced to each of these four loving influences, it's time for you to familiarize yourself with your own personal guides. Here you will find a guided meditation exercise that you can use to meet your joy guide, your doctor teacher, your chemist, and your protector. You can use the same guided meditation on separate occasions to meet each one individually. I encourage you to work with each guiding influence separately at first, until you become comfortable with each one's unique energy and method of communication. Later in the book, we will discuss ways to work with them all together. For now, use the following meditation to meet each of them. Go slowly and enjoy the experiences. Remember, if you don't get much at first, don't give up! Maybe you will see, hear, and sense your guide the first time you perform the meditation. Perhaps you will need to devote a week's worth of meditation to each guide, building on the previous experience. Keep at it, because the payoff of meeting your guides is well worth the extra effort.

Once you have completed a meditation, be sure to write down in your journal everything you can remember about the experience. If you saw one of your teachers, record what she looked like. If a guide gave you a name or any words that you recognized, write them down. If you felt a vibration change around you when you were meditating, note this. These will help you to remember and assimilate the information you receive as you work more often with each of your guides. Use a separate page for each teacher so that you can add descriptions and notes as you continue to work.

Are you ready? Let's get started!

Guide Meditation

Begin by getting comfortable and closing your eyes. Start your meditation by relaxing, grounding, and centering as in previous meditations. Surround yourself with the white light energy of the Universal Love Consciousness, knowing that this protects you in all you do in the ethereal planes. Nothing but love can come to you, and nothing but love can go from you.

Now imagine in your mind's eye a beautiful, grand staircase that rises up in front of you. There are ten steps on this staircase, and you are eager to journey upward to see what awaits you at the top. So go ahead and step up—*one*—and continue up—*two*—moving up the staircase—*three*—continuing up to the next step—*four*—climbing higher and higher—*five*—continuing up and up—*six*—moving up the stairs to the next one—*seven*—climbing higher and beginning to see the top—*eight*—continuing on and up, up—*nine*—and as you take the last step up—*ten*—you stand there and look around, relaxed and at peace.

Now see that this staircase has led you directly to your very special sacred space: your garden, your cottage in the woods, your cave, your beach. Wherever your special place is, this staircase has brought you to it once again, and you are delighted to be here. Take a few steps forward into the space, admiring all of your favorite things. As you explore, realize that there is something different today about your special place. Across from you, there stands a door, or a gate, that is closed and locked. You realize as you look at the door that you hold a silver key in your hand, and this key unlocks this new door in your special place. Know that this door is the gateway to the Other Side and that your key can unlock the door at any time. You have control over when the door is opened and over who or what comes through the door. Nothing can come through this door that you don't wish to see or experience. Know that you have the power to control everything that you encounter in the spirit world.

Now move toward this special door, realizing as you walk toward it that your joy guide (or doctor teacher, protector, or doctor chemist) is waiting on the other side of the door, hoping for admittance. If you are ready to meet your guide, go ahead and use your key to unlock the door. Open it and allow your guide to enter your space. Greet your guide in whatever way feels appropriate to you. Take a few moments to notice what sensations you are experiencing in your guide's presence. Do you feel hot or cold? Do you feel tingly or energized? Do you see anything, like a specific color? Can you see your guide's face or clothing? What is he or she wearing? What color are her hair and eyes? Can you hear anything that he says? Listen for a name, any words or phrases that you might understand. Take a few minutes now to commune with your guide and enjoy his or her presence in your life.

(Pause for five to ten minutes.)

And now it is time for you to come back to this time and place and for your guide to return to the world of Spirit. Escort your guide to the door, unlock it with your key, and allow your guide to pass back through the door and into the spirit realm. As you say good-bye, know that your guide will see you again and that you can call her in to meet with you in your special place anytime your heart desires. Your guide will always heed your call.

Now count yourself backward from ten to one, when you are wide awake and at peace, wide awake and relaxed.

15   Master Guides

During my freshman year of college, my acting teacher took a hiatus to pursue a project she was working on. A substitute came to take her place, a woman named Sherry (I have changed her name to protect the identity of the instructor), and she taught our class for the entire second quarter. Sherry was quite . . . *different.* Unlike my original instructor, Sherry didn't seem at all concerned about the art of acting. In fact, most of the stuff we did in class didn't seem connected at all to drama. Where our first instructor had us working in pairs on improvisational scenes, Sherry had the whole class forming a circle, our hands on the shoulders of the person in front of us, marching in a rhythmic ring as she chanted, "You're walking back in time." She divided us into prehistoric "tribes," and we had to decide, without the luxury of language, who was the head of the tribe, who was the medicine healer, who was the religious leader, and who filled the various other positions within the tribe. We had to invent our own language as well as perform stories for the other tribe about our customs and history. To most of us, these were strange exercises in an acting class in which we expected to interpret monologues from Ibsen or Shaw.

Over the years, I have mostly forgotten Sherry's bizarre acting classes. But one thing that has remained prominent in my memory is a meditation exercise we did early in the quarter. It changed my life forever, and for that, I owe Sherry a debt of gratitude.

I recall the class being especially rowdy that day when Sherry sat us all down and told us we needed to calm ourselves to be "in the right place" to do our work. She had us close our eyes and breathe deeply to relax our bodies. Being theatre majors, diaphragmatic breathing was something that came naturally to us, as we had to have plenty of breath support onstage to sing or to speak so the audience in a five-hundred-seat theatre could hear. As I breathed, I felt myself start to loosen up, and a sense of peace and happiness washed over me.

Then, Sherry began to take us on a guided meditation, something I had never experienced before. I had no idea where I was going or what I was doing, but my mind followed her voice eagerly, as if it had been awaiting such a golden opportunity my whole life. I pictured the forest she suggested, and I began walking through it, admiring the trees in full foliage and the azure sky that peeked through the canopy of leaves. It was beautiful, and I was as content as if I had been meditating forever.

Next, Sherry suggested that the path open onto a clearing in the woods. I stepped through a ring of trees, with a perfect circle of long, waving green grass within them, dotted with wildflowers of every color. As I heard Sherry's voice in my head suggesting that there was someone waiting to meet us, I turned to see a man standing in the center of the circle. My eyes widened, and a shiver of excitement passed through me. It was as if I had been expecting to see this man, and his presence made me tingle with anticipation.

The man was bearded, his hair and whiskers as pure white as new snow. He wore a robe of midnight blue shot through with silver threads, so he seemed to shimmer as the gentle wind stirred his garments. I saw that the robe was hooded, and he wore a dark cloak over his shoulders, held in place around his neck with an elaborate silver clasp. He stood straight and tall, almost imposing, holding a staff at his side made from a reddish wood carved with intricate designs. But even from a distance, I noted the twinkle in his dark blue eyes, and I felt an immediate trust for this stranger. He exuded warmth and love. I felt safe in his presence.

I noticed I no longer heard Sherry's voice, but I somehow understood that it didn't matter. I stepped into the long grass, feeling it brush against my hands as I waded toward him. *Who are you?* I thought as I moved, and I was more than a little surprised when I heard his immediate answer in my mind.

Merlin. I am Merlin.

I stopped walking to catch my breath. I was so stunned by his answer I couldn't help myself. Of course, I knew who Merlin was. I had started reading Arthurian literature in high school and loved every page of it, relishing the time I spent with Mary Stewart and T. H. White and their accounts of the days of Camelot. But could this be true? Could this man in my mind really be Merlin, King Arthur's most trusted advisor and the most powerful magician the world had ever known?

Or was I just getting carried away with my own imagination? Had Sherry ensnared me in one of her kooky ideas?

My eyes immediately snapped open, completely disorienting me. My classmates were still meditating, and I looked around in confusion, wondering who they all were meeting in the meadows of their minds. Certainly I must have been insane to think I had actually met Merlin the magician in my head! I waited until everyone else had finished, talking myself out of anything extraordinary that may have happened.

After class, I lingered so that I could approach Sherry in private. She smiled as I came up to her. "You're wondering about the meditation," she said immediately. "I noticed you came out of yours rather abruptly."

"I've never done that before," I stammered.

"Did it frighten you?" she asked, concerned.

"No, not at all. It was peaceful. But . . ." I hesitated. I didn't know how to ask what I needed to know without sounding insulting or stupid.

"You want to know who it was that you met, right?"

I felt my forehead furrow in consternation. "It was just a figment of my imagination, right? I made him up, didn't I?"

"What do you think?" She stared at me through her little wire-rimmed glasses, looking so wise and earnest to my eighteen-year-old eyes.

"I . . . I don't know. He feels . . . he feels right to me somehow. But that's crazy, isn't it?" I must've looked like a wild child to Sherry then, pleading with my eyes for her to confirm that I was a lunatic, that the exercise was nothing more than a silly way to get the class to calm down.

"It was one of your spirit guides," she told me firmly. "He is real. He can contact you through your dreams, through meditation." She slung her huge bag of paraphernalia over her shoulder. "Now you know who he is. What you do with that information is your choice." She smiled again and left the room.

So what did I choose to do? What most young people would: I buried the idea underneath worries about my boyfriend, my classes, and my stage roles. Every now and then, especially when I was reading another Arthurian story and Merlin showed up in the saga, I entertained the brief idea that maybe the man in the meadow I'd seen *was* real. Being the practical girl I was, though, I would push the thought aside as soon as it surfaced, and I learned to ignore the quiet yearning in my heart that wanted to explore that meditation further.

With age comes wisdom, thank Creator.

Merlin is my master guide, a great teacher from the world of Spirit. He has been my companion since I was born, and he will be with me until I make my transition, as is true of all of my guides. He possesses, however, a higher vibration than the rest of my guides, and his teachings and wisdom run deep, coming from the well of information and love that is the Universe itself. You also have a great and wise master teacher guide who walks with you on your journey.

Master guides are usually pretty easy to recognize, because their energy is much different from the other guides' energies that are around us. They usually emanate a beautiful, clear color vibration, such as white or gold or purple. Their energy is usually very high, and this higher vibration causes us to tremble or shake when we make contact with that energy. They bring with them a profound sense of calm contentment, and sometimes it is hard to disengage from their energies simply because they are so beautiful and peaceful to experience.

Master guides concern themselves with teaching and guiding us on our path to enlightenment. Most of the time, our master guide corresponds to the path that feels the most comfortable to us on our spiritual journey. For instance, a person who follows Christianity and feels comfortable in that religion might have the disciple Peter, or another saint like Theresa Avila, as his master guide. A person interested in Eastern traditions may have a master guide who walked the earth as a Buddhist monk in his incarnation. Someone of Native American descent may have a great philosopher such as White Eagle as a master guide. Or, perhaps a person needs to look at other traditions to find her path to God, and her master guide will illuminate an aspect she has never discovered before. All truths lead to the One Great Truth, the One Great Creator. How you get there, and which master guide leads you, is unimportant. It is the journey itself that counts.

Master guide energies can be confusing to some people. When I tell folks that Merlin is my master guide, they usually respond with doubt. "So you really believe that one of your guides is the Merlin from the stories?" they ask, shaking their heads. Yes, I do. I also believe that, in the case of Merlin, there were many men who filled that role at that time in history. As Marion Zimmer Bradley describes in her book *The Mists of Avalon,* I believe "Merlin" was really an office held by a wise spiritual leader, most likely a Druid. I think there were many Merlins who came and went during those times, and that my Merlin was one of those great leaders.

I think the same can be true of many master guides. If your master guide tells you he is Paul from the New Testament, is he really the Paul who wrote so many of the epistles in the Bible? Perhaps he is, or perhaps he is simply from that time period in history and was a follower of that great leader. I believe master guides can be a part of that collective energy that is Paul, or Merlin, or anyone else. Only your own master guide can tell you for sure about his identity. The main thing to remember, though, is this: in the great scheme of things, it really doesn't matter. As with all of our guides, these are simply names to call them. What matters are the messages that these beings bring to us and the help that they give us as we struggle through our challenges.

Master guides understand that our lives on earth are filled with mundane events. They support us in everything we do, and they send love and help whenever we need it. Most master guides, however, do not concern themselves with giving us messages about our day-to-day lives. If you need help making a decision about a job or you need extra energy to get through an especially long week at school, call your doctor teacher or your chemist or your joy guide to your aid. Master guides usually come through in meditations and give messages when they have a vital piece of wisdom to impart, and their words are never wasted on trivial things. They are also the only guides in our band who may work with others outside of us. Your other four guides work exclusively with you, while your master guide may lend assistance to more than one person.

Because master guide energies are so high and so powerful, it is usually a good idea to get to know your other guides before you try to get in touch with your master. When you are ready, call in your other guides and try this meditation to experience the loving presence of your own master teacher.

Master Guide Meditation

Begin by closing your eyes and grounding and centering. Take several deep breaths, and do your regular white light meditation to protect yourself as you open up to the higher realms.

Now see before you in your mind's eye the beautiful staircase that rises to the higher planes, the one with ten steps that you have climbed in the past. Start up the staircase now, knowing that with every step up, you are heightening your vibration, preparing to meet your master guide in the spirit world.

At the top of the last step, stop for a moment. In front of you stands a beautiful castle, one that shines brightly like a beacon. You feel safe and at ease as you begin to walk toward it, knowing that you will meet your wonderful master teacher when you pass through its doors.

Inside, take a moment to look at your surroundings. This is a special, sacred space in the spirit world, and you can sense the strong, nurturing energies of this place as you breathe in and out. As you stand there, taking in all of these wonderful energies, a nearby door opens, and your master teacher steps into the foyer.

What do you feel when you see your master? What does he look like? What are his garments like? Does he speak to you? What does he say? Tell your mind that you will remember every detail of this encounter, and greet your master guide in whatever way feels appropriate to you.

Take some time now to get to know your master teacher. Listen to her words, sit and ask her questions, or just bask in her presence. Her loving energy will fill your heart and make it soar.

(Take five to fifteen minutes of quiet time.)

Your master guide has brought you something today: a gift, something that you need at this time in your life. Hold out your hands so that your master can present it to you. What is it? Listen to her as she explains its significance, or remember any impressions that you receive about your gift.

Now it is time for you to return to this time and space. Walk to the door of the castle with your master teacher, knowing that you can return to this sacred place anytime you wish and that your master will be waiting for you. Say goodbye to your master however you choose, and then pass through the door and walk to the top of the staircase. As you descend, counting backward from ten to one, start to return to this consciousness. By the time you reach the number one, you are wide awake and relaxed, wide awake and at peace.

Take out your notebook and jot down any details you remember about your master guide from your meditation. Start a new page for him or her so that you can add more to it as you work further with your master.

16   Ascended Masters

Along with our own personal spirit guides, there are myriad higher energies we can choose to work with during our lifetimes. These beings often have famous names, and many of us recognize them as figures from history. Usually, they themselves were great spiritual teachers when they existed on the physical plane, and they continue to guide and influence masses of people from their positions now in the spiritual realms. Jesus, Buddha, Mohammed, Saint Germain, Kuan Yin, Mother Mary—all of these are Ascended Masters. All of them are available to us if we choose to work with them.

Now, the idea of interacting with one of the Ascended Masters might make you a little nervous. Many of us have a tendency to think things like, "I can't ask Buddha to help me with this minor issue. He's much too busy!" or "I can't really be communicating with Jesus in my meditations! He's much too important to visit someone like me." Let me assure you: *we are all loved beyond measure, no matter what*. The Ascended Masters are compassionate and understanding, and nothing pleases them more than to have us call to them for assistance. Their energies are such that they can be in many places at the same time, and they can perform astounding feats if we put our faith in them. They are never too busy to listen to us, and they will always give us wise counsel if we attune ourselves to hear their messages.

As with our master guides, we are usually drawn to certain Ascended Master energies for a reason. I have several Ascended Masters I like to work with. Jesus is a generous Ascended Master, and I often work with him when I facilitate energy-healing sessions. After all, Jesus is known to be one of the greatest healers who ever walked the earth. Another energy I enjoy working with is Kuan Yin. A Chinese goddess, she is the hearer of prayers, the compassionate mother deity of the East. Similarly, I often call upon Mother Mary (the mother of Jesus), who embodies the same sort of loving energy. These are the energies I feel most drawn to; you may have others whom you prefer to access in your own work. Just remember that all of the Ascended Masters are eager to lend their love and support to your endeavors, especially the ones that come from your heart and seek to help the world—or even just your small corner of it.

I will list here a sampling of Ascended Masters and their corresponding virtues. These are Ascended Masters whom I have worked with in the past, so I am somewhat familiar with all of these energies. This list is by no means complete, and I urge you to do more research on Ascended Masters as you are drawn to.

Aphrodite	Sexuality, marriage, romance, beauty, femininity
Babaji	Simplicity, spiritual growth, manifestation
Brigit	Healing, creativity, purpose in life
Buddha	Balance, inner peace, spiritual understanding
Horus	Clairvoyance, courage, strength
Isis	Magick, power, self-esteem
Jesus	Forgiveness, healing, direct communication with God

Kali	Protection, focus, courage
Krishna	Joy, blessings, food, relationships
Kuan Yin	Compassion, giving and receiving love, motherhood
Mary Magdalene	Independence, divine feminine, charity, unconditional love
Mohammed	Divine communication, authority, teaching, knowledge
Moses	Leadership, negotiations, clear communication, faith
Mother Mary	Children, healing, fertility, mercy
Pele	Passion, honesty, empowerment, energy
Saint Francis	Animals, career, spiritual devotion, peace, environment
Saint Germain	Spiritual purpose, transmutation, protection
Solomon	Magick, wisdom, manifestation
Thoth	Writing, teaching, sacred geometry and mathematics
Yogananda	Peace, unity of religions, divine love and communication

For more information, I recommend Doreen Virtue's book *Archangels and Ascended Masters.*

17   Angels

Quite a lot of information has been written in the last several years about angels. They have certainly enjoyed a surge in popularity in recent times, a trend that I hope will continue. I am not going to spend much time discussing angels in this book, simply because I don't want to repeat here what other sources can give you. What I do want to do is make the differentiation between guides and angels, as some folks seem to be confused about the two.

Angels are separate entities from spirit guides. Angels are incredibly powerful and wonderful spiritual beings, but they are *not* people. Your spirit guides (with some exceptions, as we will discuss momentarily) experienced a physical incarnation at some point in history. That is, they were and still are *human*. Angels are not human beings. They have never lived a physical life. Contrary to some popular thought (like the movie *City of Angels*), angels do not become human, nor do humans die and become angels. This confusion probably sprung from folks making their transitions and appearing to their loved ones after their deaths to communicate with them. The people left here on the physical plane had to explain this somehow, so they most likely assumed that their loved ones had become angels and spoke to them from heaven. Close, but no cigar! Angels are separate beings from humans, thus making them different from spirit guides.

We all have at least one guardian angel who stands with us. You can get to know your angelic guardian just as you can become familiar with your spirit guides. Your angel is most likely a protective and nurturing energy who can also work with you to accomplish your goals in life. You can call on your angel to aid in any of your everyday endeavors. Angels are attracted to beauty and truth in its many forms and manifestations. Don't ask your angel to perform a task unless you have everyone's very best interests at heart. Angels emanate pure, divine love energy, and so they cannot respond to any energy that isn't of the highest nature.

The archangel energies are some of the most powerful and loving that you can encounter. Like master guides and Ascended Masters, these angels can help you on your spiritual path and can bring sweeping changes to your life. Be prepared, though, when you seek out these energies; they will literally knock your socks off if you aren't ready for them! Archangel energies are especially useful in ritual, magick, and prayer settings. Again, there is much information available about the archangels. Here is just a short guide to their corresponding powers:

Raphael,
  Angel of the East   Communication, healing, knowledge

Michael,
  Angel of the South   Protection, courage, divine contact

Gabriel,
  Angel of the West   Messages, peace, transformation

Uriel,
  Angel of the North   Wisdom, dreams and visions, nature

For more excellent information on angels, I recommend the book *Angels: Companions in Magick,* by Silver RavenWolf.

18   Outer Band Guides

You now know that you have at least five guides who work with you throughout your lifetime, as well as one guardian angel who lends energy to you. My goodness, that's a lot of help! Actually, we're not quite finished yet. Many folks also have what we call *outer band guides*. These are guides outside of the five main guides we've already discussed. Outer band guides usually come into our lives for a specific time and purpose. When their work is done, they will often leave us, knowing that they have helped all they can with a particular issue.

For instance, suppose you inherit some money from a relative and you want to invest that money wisely. You can ask for a guide to come in to help you manage your finances and guide you to the right investment choices. Of course, it would also be wise to have a helper in the physical world, such as a broker or an accountant, who can steer you in the right direction, but your temporary guide can help you make the ultimate choices about where to put your money. Once the money is invested, this guide will most likely leave, although you can always call on his or her energy again in the future if you need to make more financial decisions.

Perhaps you are an artist, musician, dancer, or writer. More than likely, you have an outer band guide already who helps you with your chosen artistic endeavor. My husband is a writer, and he has a writing guide who helps him with his work. I sometimes do spirit artwork, which, believe me, comes directly from Spirit through me, as I can't draw a stick person to save my soul. I have an art guide, Blue Iris, who comes in and helps me with my artwork. She inspires me at times to produce spirit art, and no one is more dumbfounded than I upon seeing the finished products. It's really pretty amazing.

As a massage therapist and healer, I have several guides who help me in my practice. One of my guides, Sister Gertrude, is from a healing sisterhood on the Other Side, and she lends her energies to all healing sessions that I hold. My chemist, Black Hawk, also helps with healings, as he is a shaman and medicine man. If you do any type of healing work, you most likely already have a healing guide working with you, even if you aren't aware of her. You can get to know these guides, too, just like your inner band guides. These types of guides, who help you with your life work, will most likely stay with you until you make your transition, unless you release them yourself.

There are guides available to help you with every type of issue that you might have. Perhaps you want to be a better parent. Ask for a guide to aid you with those skills. Maybe you want to start your own business. Ask for a guide to support you in this venture. It doesn't matter what it is that you need—ask! Spirit will help you as much as possible, as long as you ask with a sincere and honest heart and work accordingly to make your dream come true. You can use the sample prayer below to call in an outer band guide for a specific purpose, or you can design your own prayer.

Divine Creator, You are the source of all love and support in the Universe. Trusting in this, I ask now that You send to me a guide who can help me with the following issue: (Take as much time as you need to explain the issue to Mother/Father

God. If it helps, write it all down and read it aloud.) I am ready to heal this part of my life, and I accept the help of this loving guide whom You will send to help me on Your behalf. I open my mind, my heart, and my inner eyes and ears to receive the messages that You have to send to me through this new guide. Thank You for Your intercession and for Your love, which transcends everything else in its beauty and depth. In the holiest name, I pray. Amen.

19   Sorting It All Out

Getting to know your spirit guides is a wonderful, exciting prospect. Actually working with them on an everyday basis, however, can be very frustrating. After all, we can't physically see or hear them, can we? It's not exactly the same as carrying on a conversation with our neighbor over the back fence or our best friend as we sit sipping tea. Everything about our guides, from their appearances to their names to the messages they impart, comes through a hazy process called mediumship. I often compare mediumship to talking on a really bad telephone connection, one where your words and what you're hearing are distorted by all the static on the line. As mediums, we often only get little bits and pieces of the sentence or the picture that Spirit is trying to send to us. This is what makes mediumship so difficult and so frustrating for most of us.

Becoming familiar with your spirit guides is sometimes like this, too. Countless students have said things like this to me: "I can see my guide. He's tall and has long, dark hair. But he won't tell me his name." Well, maybe your guide *is* trying to tell you his name and you're just not picking the information up yet. If you can see your guide when you meditate, that tells me that you have clairvoyant skills. You are getting your messages through images and pictures—

clear seeing. Perhaps your guide is trying to give you his name clair-voyantly, too. The next time you see him, notice what he's doing. Is he wearing something special? Is he holding something in his hand? Does he remind you of someone you know when you look at him? Maybe these are clues to his name. If he's wearing a Native American headdress of red feathers, maybe his name is Chief Red Feather. If he's shooting an arrow at a target, maybe his name is Swift Arrow or Straight Arrow. If he's holding a rabbit in his hands, maybe his name is Little Rabbit or Gray Bunny. If he reminds you for some reason of your cousin Michael, maybe his name is Michael. (Remember that guides can assume any appearance they want, usually choosing something we can relate to.) All of these signals can be clues to help you understand your guide better. Don't be afraid to try to interpret the clues you're receiving. Spirit will help you adjust your answers if they fall too short of the mark.

If you hear sounds, voices, or words in your meditation, you are receiving clairaudient impressions, and these could be clues to your guides and their names. What if you hear bells ringing when you concentrate on your guide? Maybe her name, then, is Silver Bell or Little Bell. Perhaps you hear an actual tune in your head when you try to connect with a guide, a song like "You Are My Sunshine." Try calling your guide Sunshine and see what response you get. As with clairvoyant images, your guides will help you to better understand the messages they send to you clairaudiently. You have to take the time to work with them, though, and try out some different names and associations.

Maybe whenever you try to meditate, you get the strong sensation of floating in water. This is impressional mediumship, or clairsentience, and it too can be a way Spirit conveys messages. Perhaps you have a guide named Gentle River or Silver Stream. Try using one of those names to call her energy to you, and see how you feel. You'll know when you're right, because it will *feel* right to you. Our guides really don't care what we call them. The names don't matter to them. They will answer no matter what. However, they will resonate to a name if you use it on a regular basis, and their vibration will be easier to access for you, so try some out with your guides. But don't get too hung up on the name game. You can always say, "Hey, you, I need help!" and they won't let you down.

Another question people often have when first getting to know their guides is, "What guide is this?" They might see a guide in meditation or hear a guide's name called to them but have no idea which guide is speaking. Is it their joy guide, protector, or doctor teacher? Again, look for clues as to what guide is coming through to you. Many Native American guides fall into the category of protectors. Many of these guides also have animal names, which denote the totem medicine in the traditions with which they work. For instance, if you see a dark bear during a meditation, perhaps you have a Native American protector guide named Big Bear or Brown Bear. Try it out. If you encounter a guide but don't know her role, ask her to show you something that relates to her job. Maybe she'll show you balloons or sunshine or flowers—all happy symbols, which might denote her joy guide status. Perhaps she comes in wearing a lab coat or holding a caduceus, the medical staff often associated with physicians. This could be a signal that she's your chemist or a healing guide from your outer band. Remember, communicating with you is new for your guides, too. Be patient with them as you work out a shorthand of symbols and words that will allow you to understand their purposes in your life.

When I first started studying mediumship, I didn't have any trouble getting to know my joy guide, my protector, and my master guide. My other guides, however, seemed rather elusive to me, and it really bothered me that I couldn't seem to get a handle on who they were. A couple of mediums had told me that I had a teaching guide named William Wilkins, so I took that name and worked with it. After a while, I started understanding that Dr. Wilkins's energy is very different from that of my more familiar guides. He is quieter and more reserved and speaks up a good deal less than Mara or Master Merlin. I became accustomed to this—after all, we all have different personalities, don't we? I couldn't expect all of my spirit guides to be flamboyant extroverts like my joy guide, or even like myself. I became very frustrated, however, because for the longest time, I couldn't get a handle on my doctor chemist at all.

I can recall going into meditations with the intention of "I want to meet my doctor chemist." I'd meditate, and sometimes I'd see flashes of a bird. I had no idea what this meant. Birds and healing didn't go together, at least not in my mind. Almost every time I tried to connect with my chemist, however, I'd see a bird. I couldn't figure it out. I couldn't even tell what kind of bird I was seeing. I thought perhaps it was an eagle because of the wingspan, but I really had no knowledge of birds, so I had no way to prove if my reasoning was right.

I struggled for over a year with this mystery, and finally I gave up. (No, it never really occurred to me to ask Spirit to show me something else or to give me my chemist in a different way. I was flying by the seat of my pants.) I thought, "Well, I know I have a chemist. I guess I'm just not supposed to know his or her name." After that, I didn't dwell on it any longer. I figured that when I needed to know my chemist, I'd be introduced in some way.

A few months later, my first spiritual teacher offered to teach trance classes at his home. Trance is a more advanced stage of mediumship, in which the medium allows her own consciousness to be displaced by a spirit. Since a spirit has no physical body and is nothing but energy, the spirit will take over the medium's body and use it to speak. I signed up, and after a couple of initial sessions, my teacher had me go into a trance state in class one night. He asked that my doctor chemist come through to speak, and without missing a beat, a voice started talking. My teacher asked who was speaking, and the voice answered, "This is Black Hawk." My teacher said, "You must be Rose's protector." He thought, since Black Hawk sounded like a Native American name, that this guide must be the protector influence in my band. Black Hawk sort of chuckled, I'm told, and answered, "No. I am what you call a doctor chemist. I am a shaman and medicine healer. I have tried to make myself known when this little one [meaning me] asked for me, but she was not receiving my messages correctly. Now she will know who I am."

After coming out of trance, did I feel stupid! I knew I had a Native American guide, and I had even been told his name had the word *hawk* in it. I also knew my protector was not Native American because I'd had an easy time getting to know Arthur. I had seen a bird in my chemist meditations, but I didn't know what kind it was. For whatever reason, I'd never put all the pieces together. Obviously, Black Hawk was trying to show me a symbol of himself, and I just wasn't picking up on it. I was certainly glad he came through in trance that evening so that I could then be confident of who he was and what purpose he served in my band of guides.

The point of this story? All of us question who our guides are and what functions they serve in our bands. Sometimes, it's difficult to sort out who's who on the Other Side. Getting to know our guides is fascinating and fabulous, but please don't become frustrated and give up if you don't get an immediately clear picture of who all of them are and what they are trying to achieve by being with you. I have a lovely spirit with me called Gentle Rain. Almost every professional medium who has read for me has picked her up *by name*, but I have never had any success in figuring out what role she plays in my life. I have come to think that perhaps she just lends a calming energy to my household, and that's why she's around. I am glad to have her influence. I just wish I knew better what to do with her. Maybe someday I will know. For now, I don't dwell on it, and I suggest to you that you don't either, when and if you find a guide to be especially elusive.

Remember, the "job descriptions" of your spirit people are just guidelines. Not all of them are going to fit into the pigeonholes we have created for them. At Camp Chesterfield, I was taught that protectors are Native American. Period. I now know that not all protectors are Native American, and I know for certain that mine is a Celtic warlord. My Native American fills the role of chemist. Your guides may fill different roles, too, and sometimes their jobs may overlap. All of your guides are protective of you. All of your guides want you to be happy. All of your guides care about your spiritual progression. As you work with them and become more comfortable with their energies, you will start to understand which guides fill which roles the best. And if you never can say for sure, "This is my joy guide" or "This is my doctor teacher," then that's OK, too. Your guides will help you no matter what title you call them by.

20   Guides of a
Different Nature

Some people may find that they have spirit guides of a wholly different nature from human beings. *Elementals* are energies that generally inhabit the natural world, but for a few folks, these energies may attach themselves as guiding influences. A very good friend of mine has a joy guide named Fairy Dancer. She is, as her name implies, of the faerie realm, but this makes her no less of a brilliant and fun joy guide. You may also have an inner or outer band guide who comes from these natural realms. Here are some of the elemental energies you may encounter as you investigate your spirit helpers.

>   *Gnomes* (also called *Brownies, Dryads, Elves, Pans,* and *Satyrs*)—
>   These entities are associated with the element of earth. They
>   usually live outdoors under rocks or tree roots or in the soil.
>   They are very concerned with the stewardship of the natural
>   world and really only associate themselves with people who
>   are kind to Mother Earth. Their energies are solid and stately
>   but very powerful when they resonate with a lucky human

being. Try connecting with these energies while meditating outside beneath a shady tree on a warm day.

Sylphs (also called *Faeries*)—These beings correspond to the element of air. They are quite beautiful and are sometimes mistaken for angels. Their wings, however, are more ethereal than angel wings, and they appear to be less substantial in weight than angelic energies. Sylphs are drawn to mental and creative pursuits and often connect with people who have similar interests. To reach your sylph guides, try meditating in a well-ventilated area, preferably outdoors, and burn some sweet incense to attract their attention.

Undines (also called *Mermaids* and *Mermen, Naiads,* and *Oreads*)—These spirits are connected to water. They closely resemble humans, unless they occupy smaller bodies of water. They are graceful and beautiful, and they are nurturing by nature. They care deeply for the soul and emotions of the human experience, as this is closely associated symbolically to the waterways that they police. Meditate near a stream, brook, or body of water to connect with your water spirit guides.

Salamanders—Corresponding to the element of fire, salamanders are thought to be the most powerful of the elementals. They can often be seen as a face or eyes in a candle flame or a fire on the hearth. They are often connected to people who have a fiery nature or who need to incorporate more passionate energy in their lives. Try focusing your eyes on a lit candle during meditation to get in touch with your salamander guides.

Summary

As you can see, we have a lot of help awaiting our call in the spirit world. Your spirit helpers, teachers, and friends want to be of use to you. Do your meditations regularly, talk to your spirit people every day as you go about your routines, and ask for their intercession when you need guidance and assistance. If you do these things with a clear, honest, and positive intent, you will be rewarded by the extraordinary relationships that blossom between you and your guides. Enjoy them!

Part 4

DIGGING IN

Now that we've met our spirit guides, we can start focusing on the process of natural and everyday spirit communication. Our guides are imperative in this, because they are the ones who help us to establish contact with those on the Other Side who wish to communicate. Our guides will also bring important information to us, which will enhance our physical, emotional, and spiritual lives. Working with our guides more closely and nurturing our feelings of affinity with them is the focus of this section.

21   Roll Call

You've learned that you have at least five spirit guides working with you. In your meditations, you've tried to get in touch with each one, and you've been recording your impressions in your journal about each particular guide. Take out your journal right now and page back through these meditations. What kinds of patterns do you see in your notes?

Do you see different colors associated with each of your guides? Perhaps only colors come through when you meditate and concentrate on connecting with specific energies. When I first started trying to get in touch with my joy guide, I always saw a splash of green. I couldn't really see her (which makes sense to me now, knowing that I am more clairaudient than anything), but I could see that green every time I tried to tune in. When I called in my doctor teacher, on the other hand, I saw the color blue instead. My protector seemed to be associated with the color red, and my master seemed to bring in the color purple. (My chemist never came in with colors. Remember, I had a hard time getting to know him.) Do you have a similar pattern that seems to emerge when connecting with your guides?

Perhaps instead of colors, you see something else: a specific animal or symbol that shows up every time you meditate on a particular guide. Remember when we talked about trying to identify your guides? Maybe if you have a protector named Black Bear, he will show you a picture of a black bear every time he's around. Your doctor chemist may show you a stethoscope, and your joy guide may show you balloons or butterflies. Find these patterns. They're probably right there in your journal already if you look hard enough for them. This kind of connection also shows you how you may be more apt to receive your messages. In this case, being shown specific pictures, you're probably more clairvoyant than anything else.

What if you haven't really seen much of anything in your meditations? Have you been writing down what you've felt? Feelings are very important, too, because they highlight clairsentient impressions from Spirit. Maybe when you've connected with your joy guide, you've felt jittery or twitchy. It could be that your joy guide's high energy vibration has affected you this way, and this is how she is trying to let you know she's around. Maybe when your master guide comes through, you feel lightheaded or spacey. Again, this can be a clue to you about which guide is trying to connect. Make sure you pay attention to these feelings, because they are important.

If you hear things in your meditations, be sure to notice what and when. Maybe snatches of a certain song indicate the presence of your joy guide or your doctor teacher. Perhaps your Native American protector comes in to the sound of drumming, or it might be that your Asian master indicates his presence with the sound of wind chimes. If you're strikingly clairaudient (you lucky devil!), your guide may simply say, "Hey, it's me!" But don't wait just for that (although you can certainly ask for Spirit to deliver these kinds of messages!). Be aware of what your guides are sending to you so that you can try to build on this communication.

Why is it so important to identify which guide is communicating? The more you understand how each of your guides communicates, the easier it will be for you to interpret their messages. It will also help you to comprehend when other energies are around you, because you will be able to strongly identify with your own guides' energies and you'll recognize strange energies when they come in.

22   Focus

By now, in working with your guides, you've probably found that you have a special affinity for a particular one. It could be any of them, but it's usually your protector, doctor teacher, chemist, or joy guide. Our master guides tend to involve themselves mostly in higher spiritual matters and aren't as concerned about our activities day in, day out.

For me, I've always had a special bond with Mara, my joy guide. I really do consider her to be one of my best friends. We seem to share a similar sense of humor, a love of pop culture, and an interest in all things Celtic. In meditations, I've been shown the past lives she and I shared together, and I believe this makes our connection even stronger. She's like a sister to me, and I can't imagine life without her. When I first started studying mediumship, she came through very strongly. As I've mentioned, I'm not especially clairvoyant, so I rarely saw her in my meditations. I did, however, see flashes of the color green and became filled with a happy, uplifting energy that I couldn't attribute to my own. When I learned her name, I realized Mara was my joy guide and the one who would work most closely with me in message work.

Take a moment now to page back through your journal. Which of your guides really sticks out? Which one seems to have an easier time coming through? Which one do you see, feel, or hear most clearly? For the majority of people, one guide jumps out and takes center stage. This guide is the one you need to focus on in the work we'll be doing over the next few pages in this book. This guide is also, more than likely, your *gatekeeper*.

Gatekeeper Guides

Your gatekeeper is one of your guides who holds a special, additional duty to his role as joy guide, chemist, doctor teacher, or protector. Gatekeepers are in charge of organizing the people on the Other Side who wish to come through and speak to you, the medium, or to a client in a reading setting. Gatekeepers work very closely with us in our message work and may become what I like to refer to as our *main message guide*. This guide will be the one who brings the most messages to you, either for yourself or for you to relay to other people. If this sounds like a big responsibility, it is. This is why it's imperative in your mediumship studies to get to know this guide as well as you know your best friend here in the physical world.

Let's try a short exercise right now. Put the book down on your lap, close your eyes, and take a few deep breaths. Now call your special guide to you, the one who you feel is coming through the easiest. You don't have to call him out loud; just use your mind, and say his name over and over a few times in your head.

He's there, isn't he? Of course he is! You just called him. It's his *job* to be there. It's his duty to come when called. Now, *where* is he? Is he standing in front of you? Is he to your right, or is he on your left side? Is he behind you? Don't think—just answer! *You're not making it up, because he is right there with you.*

All right, now you know where this special guide stands. Tell him now, in your mind, that you *always want him to stand in that very spot, every time he comes in to work with you.* If you don't like where he's standing and you'd prefer him to stand somewhere else, *ask him to move. Then tell him you want him to stand in that spot every time he comes in to work.* Yes, I'm serious. Close your eyes, feel his energy, and *tell* him in your mind. He'll listen and he'll do as he's asked. Again, it's his job.

So why is it important that you know where your guide is standing? For one thing, it establishes consistency for you as the medium. You control Spirit. Remember, in mediumship, especially in after-death communication, you will eventually be communicating with spirits with whom you are not familiar. You will need to have a way to identify who is speaking to you so that you can accurately pass on the messages to your sitter that are coming through. If you can't even distinguish between your own spirit guide and someone's dead uncle Abe, then you're not going to help anyone with your mediumship skills.

Secondly, one of the most important things in mediumship is recognizing patterns. Let's say, for example, that your main message guide and gatekeeper is your doctor teacher, Dr. Sanders. You've realized this because Dr. Sanders seems to come through very easily for you. You always know it's him because, although you can't see him very well, you always see a bucket of Kentucky Fried Chicken when he makes contact. (See what I mean about pop culture?) Now that you've assigned him a place on your right side, he always comes in to stand there, and you can feel a slight change in the atmospheric pressure when he draws near to you. He confirms that it's him by showing you the chicken. Now you know your guide is with you, and you can feel confident in consulting him about whatever it is you need.

Another way you may use your main message guide and gatekeeper is to help you identify what spirits are coming in when you begin to communicate with others besides your own. My gatekeeper is my joy guide, Mara. She always stands on my right side and speaks clairaudiently in my right ear. When we are doing messages or readings for others, she tells me who she has with her who wishes to come through. Because of the pattern she and I have established together, I *know* that if someone comes in with Mara, it is either a passed-over loved one or a joy guide. Mara never brings through any other guiding forces, because she and I have agreed that she will only bring through dead folks and joy guides. This benefits me, because it helps make identification of a spirit easier. When an unfamiliar spirit comes in while I'm working, he must first speak to Mara, who will tell me his name, his relationship to the person for whom I'm reading, or some other pertinent information. I do not speak directly to the spirit until I get confirmation from the person receiving the message that she recognizes the spirit. Then, Mara will step back, and I will communicate directly with the spirit coming through. This is another way I protect myself during readings and another way I get accurate information for those for whom I read.

All of my guides have specific places where they must stand when we are working. Dr. Wilkins, my doctor teacher, stands on my left side. If I feel another presence come up to stand with Dr. Wilkins, I know it is a doctor teacher who wishes to come through. My chemist, Black Hawk, stands behind me, and he brings through other chemists, other healers (who are often outer band guides), and other Native American guides. My master guide, Merlin, sort of hovers behind and above me, and other master teachers accompany him. My protector, Arthur, who stands out in front of me, brings other non–Native American protectors and angels in with him. Again, this is a pattern of working that I have set up with my guides, and it helps me to identify all the entities that might approach me when I work. Eventually, when you're working with all of your guides at the same time, you can do the same sort of thing if you find it useful. For now, use the shortened version of this system and start with your one special guide. Take a moment to write down in your journal where you'll be expecting that guide to stand from now on.

If you're having a problem deciding which guide you should focus on working with at this time, take a few moments to center yourself now. Sit comfortably in your chair, close your eyes, and take a few deep, cleansing breaths. Now focus your mind as if you were going into a meditation, and ask in your head, "Which guide should I work with most closely on my mediumship development?" Within a moment or two, you should get an impression or a vision or hear something indicating which of your guides would like to work with you now on your message work. *Trust the first thing that comes into your mind, because this is the right answer.* When you open your eyes, jot down in your journal the guide you'll be working with. And don't forget to tell her where you want her to stand!

Getting to Know You

Just like in every new relationship, you must learn to trust your guide, and you must adapt your way of thinking and acting to parallel the way your guide thinks and acts. This isn't as easy as it sounds. We can't see or hear our guide—at least, not in the way we can in a "regular" relationship. Think about how many times we misunderstand what a friend or family member tells us, even though we have her right here with us, where we can hear her words and see her body language, facial expressions, and gestures. When we're working with Spirit, we usually are only hearing bits and pieces of the information that is coming through. We may receive only flashes of pictures or vague feelings of happiness or sadness connected to the spirit who is trying to communicate. The misunderstandings that may come hand in hand with mediumship communication are quadrupled in number, simply because the process itself is flawed. But there are definitely ways you can work with your guide to establish a system of communication that will work for you both most of the time. This spiritual shorthand is called *symbolism.*

23   Symbolism

No matter if you are clairvoyant, clairaudient, or clairsentient, symbols will play a prominent role in your work as a medium. According to *Webster's New World Dictionary,* a symbol is "something that stands for, represents, or suggests another thing." By using symbols, Spirit can get through clear messages without using lots of words or too many confusing pictures or feelings. The challenge rests in interpreting the symbol in the right way.

Take out your journal again, and let's play an association game. Below you'll find a list of words. Copy the list into your notebook, and then clear your mind. Look at the first word on the list, and write down whatever other words that come into your mind when you read the original word. For example:

Bird

fly	blue
sing	sky
wing	tree
nest	worms

Here's your list to play with:

Dog

Sun

Cry

Mother

Death

All right. Now you've got your list and your associated words. Let's look at it again. Do any of the words on the list stand out as more positive than others? Many people may see the words *cry* and *death* as more negative words, whereas the words *mother* and *sun* might be seen as more positive. But what if you grew up in an abusive household, or your mother was an alcoholic? For someone with this background, the word *mother* might have very negative connotations. Look closely at your list. Are any of your associated words due to past experiences that have been ingrained in you?

Really, all of the words you came up with as associations are there because of your past experiences. Each of us is unique. No list is going to exactly match another, because we all have different experiences that we bring to an exercise like this. For instance, the word *dog,* to me, is associated with loyalty, bravery, humor, playfulness, and companionship. I love dogs. I can't imagine not having one in my life. In my experience, dogs have brought nothing but happiness. Thus, the words I associate with *dog* will always be positive ones.

If that word were *chicken,* however, it would be a different story. When I was a small child, my father took me to visit a friend of his who lived on a farm. This man gave me a bucket of corn so that I could feed his chickens. I remember being totally surrounded by these flapping, noisy birds and being a little afraid. Unfortunately, one of the chickens decided I wasn't handing out the food fast enough, and she flew right up into my face to try to get at the feed. I dropped the bucket, which agitated the other chickens. In a matter of moments, I was caught in the middle of a chicken fray, and I was screaming for my father, absolutely petrified. To this day, I remember that terrible fear. Needless to say, I'm not a big fan of chickens. I'm sure the words that I would list in association with *chicken* wouldn't be very flattering at all.

What's the point here? In working with symbolism, it's vitally important to remember your own experiences. When you see a symbol in a message, you are going to automatically associate that symbol with something specific. If you receive a chicken as a symbol, perhaps you'll automatically think of picnic dinners with your grandma. I, however, would think of being frightened as a child, and my first impulse would be to ask the person I was reading for if he also had a frightening experience in his childhood. It's imperative, however, that *you* know what the symbol means and that it means the *same thing* every time you see it.

This consistency in symbolism is important for your development. Whenever I see the American flag in a reading, I know that someone is coming through who had a connection to the military. Sometimes, I'll get the exact branch of service the person was in, sometimes not. But that flag is a glaring symbol to me of military service. My guides know not to bring an American flag to me unless the person who wants to come through was in the service, because that is the meaning I am going to ascribe to that flag. How do my guides know this? Because we've worked together for quite a while now, and in meditations we've agreed on certain symbology that they can use to send messages. We're going to talk about how to do that in just a moment. Remember now that the consistency factor in interpreting symbols is vital. If you have to change symbols all the time, it makes for harder message work with more interpretation errors.

Certain people may also become symbolic for use in your mediumship work. When someone who has passed over comes through in a reading for a client, I'll often get the spirit's name. Sometimes, though, I don't hear it, and I will ask the spirit (through Mara) to identify the relationship he or she has with the sitter. Usually, I'll just get an impression of this (clairsentience), and I'll feel that the relationship is mother, grandmother, cousin, father, et cetera. If I don't get this knowing sense, though, I might see instead a picture of my own grandmother, my own mother, or my own deceased friend. I've learned these are symbols from Spirit to tell me who is coming through. I know it's not my own dead relatives trying to horn in on the reading. Why on earth would they be interested in talking to one of my clients, a complete stranger to them? This is one good way for a spirit to tell me what its relationship is to the sitter, and it works very well for me. Maybe it'll work well for you, too.

Using pictures of celebrities is another way Spirit has brought through information in my readings. Usually, I'll hear names very clearly called out to me, but there have been occasions (we all have them!) when my clairaudient ears didn't seem to be working quite as well as normal. On one such occasion, when I was giving messages to my church congregation, I saw a flash of the actor George Clooney. The only thing I could think of was that someone named George wanted to speak, and sure enough, the George who came through from Spirit desperately wanted to talk to his daughter in the congregation. I don't have anyone close to me named George, so Spirit chose this famous actor's picture, knowing I'd be able to identify it. Since then, I've seen George Clooney in a lot of readings. I'm sure some of my female clients would like to hear that George Clooney is coming into their lives soon. Unfortunately, he's just a symbol for me.

Your personal symbology will evolve over time. Mediumship is a process, as I've pointed out many times, and your communication with Spirit will grow and change as you work. Symbolism, one of the primary ways that Spirit communicates, will become more familiar to you as you work with your main message guide and decide what system of communication is best for the both of you.

Universal Symbolism

In talking about symbolism, we must acknowledge the great body of *universal symbolism* that is available to us. Universal symbolism has evolved over many, many years, and it can play a large role in your mediumship communication. One symbol that has become universally known over the latter part of the twentieth century is the peace sign. According to Internet sources, this symbol was first used in 1956 by the Campaign for Nuclear Disarmament. During the late sixties, the sign was adopted by many people in the counterculture movement to denote resistance to the war in Vietnam and commitment to peace. It is now a symbol that most people, no matter what their background, ethnicity, or gender, associate immediately with peace. This is what makes it a universal symbol.

Over the next few pages, I'll give you a list of universal symbols. This list is important, because your guides in the spirit world have already been trained to use this kind of symbolism when trying to communicate with the physical world. Becoming familiar with the symbols on this list can only help to enhance your mediumship skills. Is this list the be-all and end-all of symbology? I should hope not! Remember that symbology is ever-evolving and that your personal interpretation and experience are going to color even the most universal of symbols. Ultimately, the important thing is for you and your guides to decide which symbols will be used for effective communication. This list is just a starting point. Before you start reading about the universal meanings of some symbols, do the exercise below.

Symbol Exercise #1

Get out your journal. Take a few deep breaths to center yourself and, in your mind, call in your main message guide. Tell your guide it's time to work. Then, look at the following list of symbols. Copy each word into your journal, clear your thoughts, concentrate only on that word, and then scribble down anything that comes into your mind. Don't worry about how you're arriving at the associations; just write down your impressions, the words you hear, or the pictures you see. Then, when you're finished with all of the words, go on and read the lists of universal symbols. See if any of the impressions you got (with the help of your guide) are similar to the meanings listed here. Work with this list of symbols:

The color red

The color blue

A cave

Amethyst (the stone)

Bear

Wolf

Butterfly

A babbling brook

Colors

Colors are very important symbols in mediumship work. Always try to note what color something is, because the color symbology, combined with the object itself presented as a symbol, can be a powerful and accurate message from Spirit. Naturally, there are many differing hues within the spectrum that won't be addressed on this list. If you like using color symbolism and you find it easy to communicate with your guides this way, the vast array of color will be something extra that you should explore. For now, use the list below as a way to get to know the symbology of color.

Beige—Neutrality, indecision, diplomacy

Black—Transformation, change, ending of a cycle

Blue—Inner peace, spirituality, spiritual love, devotion, healing

Brown—Depression, muddy thoughts, connection to earth

Gold—Higher thoughts and mind, spiritual advancement, wisdom, divine masculine

Gray—Uncertainty, hesitation, confusion, depression

Green—Fertility, growth, prosperity, harmony, balance

Indigo—Powerful and high spiritual vibration, esoteric initiation, connection to higher mind and other worlds

Orange—Creativity, confidence, removing fear and inhibition, blend of desire and mind

Pink—Sensitivity, tenderness, self-love

Red—Power, physical force, sexual energy, passion, temper, anger, desire

Rose—Self-love; unconditional, spiritual love

Silver—Psychic abilities, intuition, reflection, illusion, divine feminine

White—Divine energy, purity, grace, spiritual attainment and power

Yellow—Intellect, reason, mental stimulation, rational thinking

Stones, Gems, and Metals

Stones, jewels, and other earth offerings can be important symbols in mediumship work. They often denote spiritual growth, attainment, and awareness. They are sometimes associated with a specific Ascended Master or entity whom you may choose to work with or to tell your client about if reading for someone else. Past life associations with certain cultures and civilizations may also be revealed through stone symbology. If you are clairvoyant and can actually see the stone, be sure to note if it is cut and shiny. If so, this symbolizes a refined soul attribute. If the stone is uncut or in its raw form, it means that progress in spiritual matters is still in development.

- **Amethyst**—Psychic ability and energy, connected to Atlantis and Saint Germaine

- **Diamond**—Attainment, transmutation, the archangel Michael

- **Emerald**—Cosmic awareness and healing, the archangel Uriel

- **Gold (metal)**—Connected to Father God, great wisdom, power through knowledge

- **Ivory**—Attainment; control of desire; connected to Atlantis, Lemuria, and India

- **Jade**—Spiritual energy melding with physical, life force, connected to the Orient

- **Lapis**—Facilitated spiritual growth, connected to Egypt, magick

- **Pearl**—Growth through suffering and hard work, astral gifts, clairvoyance, clairaudience, Master Jesus

- **Ruby**—Highest earth attainment, power of human spirit, heart chakra

- **Sapphire**—Higher mind, understanding of higher laws, the archangel Gabriel, Ascended Masters Jesus and Moses

- **Silver (metal)**—Connected to Goddess traditions, intuition, moon cycles, fertility

- **Turquoise**—Connected to Atlantis and Native Americans, attunement to spirit world

For more information concerning stones and minerals, I highly recommend the book *Love Is in the Earth*, by Melody.

Earth Symbols

A variety of information can be gleaned from earth symbols that appear as messages. As you'll see after reading through the following list, earth symbols don't have any overlying common meanings, but they usually do symbolize specific situations when they come up in a message. See if you can figure out from these earth symbols why they stand for what they do.

Water—Emotions; a emotional situation; notice if the water is calm, choppy, and so forth to ascertain deeper meanings

Glacier (ice)—A large, emotional issue; frozen emotion

Boulder(s)—Obstacles

Cave (passageway)—Initiation, passage from one stage to another, security

Desert—Barrenness, a dry spell, hidden growth

Mountain—Higher attainment, spiritual attainment, higher states of consciousness

Plateau—A time of assimilation, integration, reassessment

Sand—Changes, shifts in perception, shaky foundations, something temporary

Animals

Like its counterpart symbol of water, animals are often symbolic of our emotional states. One thing to specifically watch for with animal symbology is whether the animal is contained. If it is caged, it can mean symbolically that emotions are repressed or that someone is not expressing his emotions in the best way. Gauging the animal's temper is also important in interpreting the symbol. Is the animal calm and relaxed, or is it agitated? This can help to further explain or narrow down the symbolic meaning of the message coming through.

Animals are also very important in Native American traditions. Native Americans believe that each animal contains vital energy, or medicine, and that these medicines can teach us a great deal about our world and ourselves. Knowing more about the Native American connections to animal medicine can help interpret symbols that come through in your messages. One book that may be helpful to you is *Animal Speak,* by Ted Andrews.

Lastly, animals used symbolically can point to a spirit guide or totem animal for either you (if you're getting messages for yourself) or the person you're reading for. Some people may have Native American guides who work with them, and these guides often have names that honor their animal medicines, like my Black Hawk, or my sons' Little Turtle and Spotted Pony. This animal symbol may give you a double meaning: a name for a spirit guide and an important energy that needs to be recognized.

Here are just a few animals and their meanings:

Bear—Introspection, retreat, great wisdom, mothering/nurturing instincts

Cat—Independence, aloofness, magick and mystery, connected to ancient Egypt

Horse—Personal power, progress, motivation, vehicle for self-expression

Lion—Protection, vigilance, pride, willpower

Rabbit—Fertility, fear, timidity

Snake—Initiation, clairvoyance, power, deception (especially if hidden in grass)

Spider—Creativity, manipulation, can indicate needed caution

Wolf—Teacher, group orientation, pathfinder

If a symbolic animal has wings, it is often an indication of mental thought patterns. In these cases, the nature of the beast refers directly to the nature of the thoughts.

Bee—Industry, workaholic, telepathy, wisdom, feminine principles

Beetle—Occult wisdom, connected to Egyptian life

Bugs (general)—Irritating conditions, illnesses

Butterfly—Transformation, changes, higher intuitive abilities

Eagle—Great spiritual achievement, daring, bravery, initiative

Fireflies—Intermittent psychic energy, bursts of clarity

Hawk—Clairvoyant abilities, searching for answers

Hummingbird—Great joy, alignment of all bodies

Insects (general)—A group or mass mentality

Ladybug—Good luck, protection for youngsters, domestic situations

Mosquitoes—Gossip, malicious thoughts

Peacock—Vanity, egotism, eyes on feathers can mean clairvoyance

Poisonous insects (general)—Poisoned thoughts

Other Common Symbols

Over the years I've been working as a medium, I've developed my own personal shorthand of symbols that I use with my guides. Some of these symbols and their meanings have come from my study of tarot; some have come from dream interpretation; some just make sense to me, so I use them in my work. To give you a starting point, I thought it might be helpful to list some of these for you. Work with this list, and the universal symbology lists, to see if you like them. If the symbols and the meanings resonate with you, encourage your guides to use them when you work together. If a particular symbol doesn't work for you, see if you can come up with another one that can substitute for that particular meaning.

American flag—Military service

Badge—A police officer or someone involved in law enforcement

Bible—May indicate a minister or a very religious person

Cake—An upcoming birthday or anniversary (wedding, death date, or other)

Candle—Prayers. If the candle is lit, the prayer energy is being heard. If unlit, someone needs to pray for guidance and assistance, because Spirit wants to help.

Car—Often the person receiving the message. Can symbolize his or her journey in the material world. Can also indicate a new car or a problem with a car.

Fire—A person born under a fire sign in the zodiac (Aries, Leo, Sagittarius). Can also indicate a person with a fiery temper. Rarely portends an actual fire or a need to be careful of fire.

House—Another symbol of the person receiving the message. Can represent the person's physical body. Look to see if the house is well maintained or in need of repair.

Numbers—Numbers can symbolize time periods (three months, three weeks, three days). They can indicate a month of the year (3 = March), or the day of a month. See what other information comes in with the number to better understand its context.

Rosary—Roman Catholicism, prayer. May indicate someone in the priesthood or other holy orders (nun, deacon, and so on).

Roses—Messages of love from Spirit. Look to see if there are thorns on the stem. If thorny, the person sending love may not have been able to express his feelings when he was still in the body. Note the color of the rose for a further message from Spirit.

Tornado—Chaotic energy surrounding the situation or person. The need for calm and balance is great.

Now that you have some idea about how symbolism works, do the following exercise to get more comfortable with your main message guide.

Symbol Exercise #2: The Weather Report

Sit comfortably in your meditation space. Light it the way you like, play soothing music, and burn some incense if it helps you to relax. Take a few deep breaths to center and balance yourself. In your mind, call to your guide and tell her it's time to work.

When you feel your guide come to her position around you, greet her and tell her you want to work on predicting the weather. Go through a few weather conditions in your mind: see a bright sun; see fluffy, white clouds; see stormy, gray rain clouds; see a snowy scene; see a hard rain falling; see a misty, light shower. Allow each of these scenes to play in your mind for a few moments.

Now address your guide by name. Tell her these are the symbols you'd like her to use when you ask her for the next day's weather report. Ask her for some type of confirmation that she understands.

If you are not clairvoyant and feel more comfortable with hearing or feeling your messages, give your guide directives about working in those ways. For instance, tell her you want her to use the word *sunny* if the day is to be clear and warm. Tell her to use the word *shower* for a light rain and the word *stormy* for a heavy downpour. If you tend to be more clairsentient, tell your guide to bring you a feeling of heat for a hot day and a chilly feeling for a cold one. Tell her to represent a wet day by causing a shiver up your back. You get the idea:

establish your shorthand with your guide so that she can get a clear, easy-to-interpret message to you.

Finally, thank your guide and tell her that you'll begin now by predicting the weather together for the next day. Wait. What is the first thing you feel, hear, or see? It should be one of the symbols you've just established with your guide. If it doesn't come right away, address your guide again by name and ask her to bring you a message about the weather for tomorrow. Be firm and specific, and then remember the first thing that comes in—a thought, a word, a noise, a feeling. Thank your guide for her assistance.

Make a new entry in your journal. Be sure to date it, because when you check the accuracy of your predictions, you'll want to be positive you're looking at the correct date.

Be sure to follow up on your exercise by checking the weather the next day. See how close you and your guide come to predicting the next day's weather. Who knows? Maybe you have a future in meteorology.

Do this exercise once a day for at least a week, and record all the results in your journal.

So how did you and your guide do on this exercise together? If you had a tough time getting messages, be patient. Remember that this is really one of the first times you've worked with your guide on a specific question or issue. It will take time for her, and you, to get comfortable with the process.

What if you got several accurate predictions but each time your guide used different symbols from the ones you established? Well, you obviously were able to interpret the symbols she gave you. Maybe her symbols will work better than the ones you thought up. If you like the symbology she used, then why not incorporate it? Ask her to keep using it.

What if all of your predictions over a week's time were wrong? Well, there are a couple of things to consider here: First, again, this is a new process. You've got to be patient with yourself and with

Spirit. To use an earlier analogy, I didn't really like riding a bicycle the first time I climbed onto one. I ended up with several bumps, bruises, and cuts from the falls I took that day. But I was determined to learn to ride a bike, and eventually I prevailed. So will you, if you keep your will to learn prominent in your mind and keep your heart open to Spirit's help.

Secondly, are you sure your predictions were that off? Now, if you predicted your town would be hit by Hurricane Alvin and instead forty inches of snow dumped from the sky, this is an inaccurate prediction. However, don't overlook the fact that a day is twenty-four hours long. Did you predict it would rain, only to have a clear sky taunt you outside your workstation window? What happened during the night, though? Did you notice that when you took the dog outside for his morning ritual at six a.m., the grass was wet and shiny? There's your rain! Is this cheating? Not by a long shot. You didn't specifically tell your guide that you wanted a weather prediction just during the workday, did you? Maybe you need to be more specific with your particular guide. Still, in psychic work, we'd call that a hit: you predicted rain, and it did rain.

The more you work with your guide on establishing symbolism in your message work, the easier you will receive messages and the more accurate and reliable those messages will be. Do you need to sit down and go over symbolism with your guide before you ask for a prediction? Not always. You may want to see what symbols your guide will come up with for you to use and then decide whether those symbols work for you or not. Sometimes, a symbol may seem kind of obscure. Let's say you tell your guide to give you a prediction for the weather on Saturday morning, and she keeps showing you a mug of steaming coffee. *What does this mean?* you think. You're not a coffee drinker, and what could coffee have to do with weather? Finally, you give up, only to discover on Saturday morning when you wake up that the temperature outside has dropped about thirty degrees. Frost coats everything, and when you take the dog for a walk, the air is blustery with a snowy chill. When you finally get back inside, you reach for the teakettle before you even take off your jacket, daydreaming about a nice, hot cup of tea to warm you up . . .

Tea. Coffee. Steaming mug. Cold morning. Eureka! You now know what your guide was trying to tell you through her symbolism. It was you who interpreted that mug to be filled with coffee. Whether coffee or tea, what the steaming mug stands for in relation to weather is very apparent: you're going to need something hot to drink on a cold morning like this one. So even the most obscure symbols can be interpreted, and sometimes this is what we must do when Spirit sends us a message.

Keep predicting the weather with your guide, and add a couple more prediction exercises to your daily conference and journal entry.

Symbol Exercise #3: The Stock Market

You don't need to know anything about Wall Street or dollar-cost averaging to do this exercise with your guide. Get a newspaper and turn to the financial section. Find the stock listings and skim through them. Pick out a stock that you'd like to track; it doesn't matter which one it is. Make an entry in your journal with the date, the stock name, its abbreviation, and the price of the stock that day. Next, take a few moments to breathe and center. Focus your mind, call in your guide, and tell her it's time to work. Concentrate on the stock name in your mind, and ask your guide to tell you if the stock's price will close the day up or down from its opening price. Wait and interpret the answer that comes to you. Be sure to write that down in your journal, too. Thank your guide for her help. Do this exercise for at least a week, tracking your specific stock and how accurate your predictions are. Do you have a future in the stockbroking world?

Symbol Exercise #4: First Call

For this simple exercise, sit and breathe to relax yourself. Call in your guide, tell her it's time to work, and ask her, "Who will be the first person to telephone me tomorrow?" What's the first thing that comes into your mind? Write it down, even if it doesn't seem to make sense. Date your journal entry so you can see what came through.

The next day, pay very close attention to the telephone. When it rings for the first time, answer it and note who is on the other end. Did your guide send you the right information? If your caller is very different from the prediction, see if there are any similarities between the projected caller and the real one. Also see if you can make any connections between the actual caller and the symbol your guide brought to you.

I remember doing this exercise a long time ago and getting a picture of a housefly in my mind when I asked Mara this question. I repeated the question, and I got the fly again. Frustrated, I mumbled to myself, "Great. Jeff Goldblum [from the remake of the movie *The Fly*] is going to call me. Right." The next day, my first phone call was from some kind of salesman. Not exactly a housefly, true, but definitely as annoying as one! Like I said before, sometimes the associations can be obscure but meaningful. Maybe from then on, a housefly (or whatever symbol your guide chooses for you) will indicate a salesperson in your readings. Try doing this exercise for a week and see what results you get.

Summing Up Symbolism

By doing these exercises, you should become a bit more familiar with your main message guide, and you should begin to understand some of the symbolism that your guide will use for message work. Make sure that you write down in your journal all of the symbolism that comes through to you. It's probably wise to start a separate section in the journal just for symbols. Remember, your interpretations of the symbols are just as important as the universal meanings that may be ascribed to them. Compiling your own symbol dictionary in your journal will help you immensely as you continue to broaden your spirit communication skills.

24   Dreams and Dreamwork

I have had very vivid dreams while sleeping ever since I was a child. Some were breathtakingly beautiful and felt as real as the pillow under my head; some were obviously dreamscapes where I could act out fantasies. Some, especially when I was a little girl, were nightmares filled with dark and scary images. Even so, I always looked forward to sleeping at night, because although I was young, I still knew, somewhere deep in my soul, that my dreams were a portal to other worlds.

This is a great truth. Dreams open up our consciousness to other planes, other realms, and other states of mind. Learning to use our dreamtime to access these other states is fascinating and complex work. Here, we will explore one part of it, which helps us to communicate with our guides, teachers, and loved ones in the spirit world.

Have you ever dreamt of someone you love who has passed away? What can you remember about the dream? If you're like a lot of people, you remember the details with tremendous clarity. You probably recall the colors around you, the feeling of the atmosphere, and how clearly you heard your loved one's voice when he spoke to you. If hard pressed, you'd most likely admit that the dream felt . . . well, it felt *real*.

It felt real because it *was* real.

Many people have experienced exquisitely tangible dreams. When a loved one appears like this, it isn't really a dream at all. The sleep state has allowed the conscious mind to open further, giving it first-hand access to the spirit planes. An appearance of a loved one similar to those described here is, in actuality, a *visitation*.

Visitations happen to many, many people. In their groundbreaking book *Hello from Heaven!*, Bill Guggenheim and Judy Guggenheim include nearly twenty accounts of what they call *sleep-state ADCs (after-death communications)*. They are all characterized by an undeniable knowledge on the part of the dreamer that the encounter with the deceased was real and amazingly vivid. All of the visitations were positive and filled with loving feelings, another characteristic that marks the validity of these visions. I know that I can personally attest to the reality of after-death communication via dream visitations.

My mother passed away in May 2000, the victim of a massive coronary that took her immediately. Her death was a stunning blow to my family, and despite my firm belief in Summerland and after-death communication, I mourned her deeply. I longed for messages from her, thinking that she would most certainly come through one of my medium friends very quickly. That, unfortunately, did not happen. I waited almost six months before I got a message from my mother through a medium. She did visit me twice, though, in dreams. Those appearances helped to assure me that she was safe and well.

In the first dream, which took place about six weeks after she died, I saw the house where I grew up. The dining-room table was set for a feast, and my whole family was gathered around it. My mother loved to entertain, and her pride and joy was her cooking. She was highly insulted if you came into her house and didn't devour everything she put in front of you. I stood in the kitchen, looking in on the scene through the half-wall that divided the kitchen and dining room. I could feel my husband standing behind me, and my mother was by the sink, removing an apron that she was wearing. She turned toward me at the same time that my husband came up behind me and put his arms around me, hugging me to his chest. My mother smiled and pulled us both forward into her embrace. I could feel her cheek pressed against mine, and the rough texture of her worn fingertips brushed over the skin on my arms. I sank into her touch, feeling the absolutely unquestionable strength of her love for my husband and me. It enveloped us like a warm blanket, and I felt at peace for the first time since her death.

Her second visitation occurred about six months later. I was in a place that looked familiar, yet strange. It seemed to be a department store I had frequented all my life, but the colors and the light were almost blinding. As I turned in a slow circle, trying to figure out where I was, my mother stepped out from behind a counter. She looked stunning: her hair was styled in loose waves around her youthful face; her skin glowed with health; her smile dazzled. She took me by the hand and asked me what I wanted for Christmas. I realized as she asked me that her lips did not move: she was speaking to me telepathically. It was then that I remembered that my mother was dead, and a terrible feeling of loss welled up inside me. I threw my arms around her and cried, "You, Mom. For Christmas, I want you back." Again, I heard her words in my mind: "I know you do, but I can't do that. But you know I'm always here. You know that." She held me for a long time, and I could still feel the weight of her arms around me when I awoke.

These visitations from my mother fit the scenario of dream-state after-death communications. Both were realistic and straightforward, moving in a logical fashion from point A to point B in the dream. Both were positive experiences in which I sensed the deep love and compassion my mother brought to me. Both dreams are as bright in my memory today as they were when they occurred. These three characteristics can help you determine if your dreams are just dreams or if they are actual visitations from your loved ones in Spirit.

Visitations from spirit loved ones happen to many people, but they don't happen frequently. As I mentioned, in the years since my mother passed away, I've only had two visitations from her, and these both occurred in her first year (in our time measurement) in the spirit world. I have had countless dreams about my mother, though, which are nice, but I know they are not visitations. Most of these are typical dreams—usually pleasant but kind of strange, a bit confusing, and they leave me with a vague, hazy feeling when I awaken. You have probably also had dreams like these about your loved ones in Spirit. These are *not* visitations, nor are any dreams you have about your loved ones that are negative in any way. Scary dreams can be hard to understand, but these types of dream are valuable, too.

About ten months after my mother passed, I had a very disturbing dream. I was standing in the backyard of my parents' house on a cold, dark day. I didn't like being out there, because I knew my mother had died in the backyard. As soon as this thought crossed my mind, I noticed a large pile of leaves at the foot of a tree. I suddenly realized that my mother was under that pile of leaves, and she wanted me to come and find her. Repulsed, I tried to back away, but my feet stuck to the ground, making it impossible to move. Terror seized me, and I frantically tried to get away from the leaves as they started to rustle. I knew that at any moment my mother was going to burst out of that pile. More than anything, I didn't want to see her when that happened.

I remember waking up from that dream absolutely terrified. That feeling of horror was completely different from the feelings of love and assurance I'd had after the other two dreams of my mother. Why was this dream so different? Was this some kind of terrible visitation?

Absolutely not. This type of negative dream experience is simply the mind's way of working through anxiety. All of us have issues with our loved ones, no matter how important they were in our lives. My relationship with my mother, although mostly good, was not always perfect. Whose is? We all fight with our parents; all of us deal with our upbringing and try to struggle through our own life challenges, bearing forward, for good or ill, the morals and values that our parents have instilled in us. In this dream, and in the ones like it that you may have had about your loved ones, we struggle to make amends with passed family and friends. Depending on your relationships, you may be dealing with feelings of remorse, anger, abandonment, or resentment. Any of these residual feelings can cause your subconscious mind to worry about them in the dream state, thus conjuring up a scary or bad dream as you try to reconcile these feelings. These dreams are *not* visitations, showing a hell that a loved one is enduring. In reality, they hold up a mirror to your own personal challenges that you are trying to resolve.

Dreams can help us to understand the passage of our loved ones into spirit, and they can give us a glimpse of what life on the Other Side is like for them. I am convinced that my second visitation from my mother allowed me to see a bit of what Summerland looks like. Because clairvoyance is not my most developed spiritual sense, I have not had the opportunities that some mediums talk of to see the spirit world. The visitation from my mother enabled me to experience a taste of life in Spirit. The blinding colors and lights convinced me that it really was the Other Side, for this corresponds to what many people have described in their own near-death experiences, channelings, and dreamwork. You too can ask your loved ones to visit you in your dreamtime. Try the exercise below to encourage contact with your loved ones.

Dream Exercise #1: Contact with a Loved One

Before you go to sleep at night, place your journal next to your bed or put a tape in your recorder and set it where you can reach it immediately upon awakening. Before you lie down to sleep, close your eyes and prepare yourself as if going into a meditation. Instead, call your gatekeeper guide to you in your mind. Quietly tell him that you would like to visit Summerland in your dreamtime and see your loved one. Choose one loved one whom you'd like to visit, and hold that person's name, face, and personality firmly in your mind as you talk to your guide. Then affirm to yourself out loud, "I easily access the spirit world to visit _____ [fill in your loved one's name], and I easily remember the entire experience immediately upon awakening." Thank your guide, and go on to sleep.

As soon as you wake up, take your journal and write down your experiences, or turn on your recorder and tape what you experienced.

You must write down or record your experiences *as soon as you wake up*. Otherwise, you'll risk forgetting the experience you had. If you wake up at 3:45 a.m. and say, "Oh, what a cool dream about Mom! I'll write it all down in the morning," I guarantee you won't be able to remember half of what happened by the time you get up three hours later. If you sleep with a partner and don't want to disturb him or her, crash on the couch for a few days. You'll both get what you need from your dreamtime.

What if, on the first night you try, nothing happens? You don't remember any dreams at all. Be diligent, and don't give up. It might take a few days, or even a few weeks, for you to receive a visit from your loved one. Why? Because your loved one might be new to the whole process of visiting, and it may take her a while to get the hang of it. It may also take a while for your guides to help program your body to open up to the spirit world and remember its experiences. Be patient with your guide, with your loved one, and especially with yourself, and you'll see results.

Dreamwork between the Worlds

Besides seeing your loved ones who have passed away, your dreamtime can also help you in your spiritual studies. When we are asleep, our consciousness can leave our bodies and we can travel to other planes in order to learn. Our consciousness stays attached to our bodies by the *silver cord*, which is a thin but strong energy line, like the umbilical cord that attaches a fetus to its mother in the womb. At death, our consciousness leaves our bodies to travel to the Other Side, but this time it cannot return to the body because the silver cord has been severed. While alive, you can never become "lost" in the astral planes, because the silver cord will always draw you back to the physical body.

When we sleep, we can travel to other planes with our guides and teachers to learn about these other dimensions. We can also ask questions about our lives and assimilate the answers we receive. When you think about the possibilities of what we could be doing in our dreamtime, the scenario is staggering. With God, all things are possible, and when we can learn to use our minds (and the dream state is part of the mind), then think of what we could accomplish. Start building your own knowledge by trying the following exercise.

Dream Exercise #2: Going to School

Again, before you go to sleep, be sure to have your journal or your tape recorder handy. This time, calm yourself and call to your gatekeeper guide, as well as to all of your other guides. As you feel them gather around you, tell them all that you wish to meet with them in your dreamtime to explore the other planes of existence. Affirm out loud to yourself, "I easily access my guides and teachers during my dreamtime, and I remember everything that we do together as soon as I awaken." Thank your guides, tell them you'll see them in your dreams, and go to sleep.

Again, be sure to record your impressions *immediately* upon awakening. If you don't recall anything the first few times you try this exercise, don't give up. Keep working with your guides on this, and you'll see results.

The results of this exercise may be very different for every person. Some may explore the other planes, seeing what life on the Other Side is like. Others may go directly to a classroom (which can look like a classroom, or it could be by a river, in a house, or anywhere else) and receive instruction from their guides. *Don't discount anything that you receive when working with this exercise. Write down everything you remember.* A lot of the information you receive may be symbolic. Look hard at the images, words, and feelings you receive while asleep to uncover the deeper symbolic meaning these messages may hold.

Dreams can hold the answers to questions we need to ask. Perhaps we need guidance concerning a job offer or we are contemplating a move. Why not ask for information about the situation from your guides via your dreams? Sometimes, messages are easier to give and receive through the dream state because we are more open energetically. For help with a problem, try the exercise below.

Dream Exercise #3: Assistance, Please

Again, before retiring, have your journal or tape recorder nearby. Close your eyes and relax. Call your guides to you, and tell them that you would like to use your dreamtime to answer a question you have. Say, "I ask that you send me messages about the following situation during my dreams tonight." Take as long as you need to explain the situation to your guides, and be sure to stay focused on the question as you go through it. Then say, "I affirm that I receive messages concerning this question in my dreamtime, and I remember everything from my dreams as soon as I awaken." Thank your guides and go to sleep.

When you wake up, write down everything you remember *immediately.* You don't have to take the time to analyze the dream right then; just be sure to write as much down as possible. Then, in the morning, when you are feeling more alert, read through what you wrote about the dream. Look at the overall feeling the dream brought to you. Were you happy? Calm? Angry? Scared? This feeling is a big indication of what outcome may be awaiting you regarding your question. Look at each piece of the dream individually, and try to analyze the components symbolically. Use the symbols list that you've been working on with your spirit guides. If there's something present that you've never encountered in symbolism before, you may want to use a dream symbology book. As with all symbolism, however, remember that the meanings must resonate with you. If they don't, examine your own thoughts and meditate on the symbol. A meaning will come to you, especially if you ask your guides for assistance. Put all the symbolic meanings together, and see what you can make of your dream.

How about an example to see how this works? Say that you are thinking about starting a family. You and your husband have talked about it, and you know that you are both very much in love and want to have children. However, you're not convinced the timing is right for a baby. Your husband is still in school, and your job doesn't pay as much as you would like to accommodate a new addition. You ask your guides to help you in your dreamtime with this issue.

You dream that you are having breakfast. You sit at a well-appointed table, and you notice a centerpiece vase of beautiful spring flowers. Your mother enters the room and puts a plate of eggs in front of you. She smiles and brings you a glass of orange juice. As you start eating, you feel the sunshine coming in the window next to the dining room table.

When you wake up, you write down the main symbols in your dream. Your list looks something like this:

Table

Spring flowers

Mother

Eggs

Orange juice

Sunshine

What could all this mean? Well, a table, especially a well-appointed one, can be symbolic of a happy home and family life. The flowers may mean love, growth, and fertility; they can also be symbolic of the springtime itself. Mothers correspond to nurturing and motherhood in general, and eggs often symbolize a new beginning or a possible birth, whether an actual birth or a figurative one. Orange juice is filled with vitamin C, which could indicate something concerning health, and the color orange is connected to creativity or creative forces. Sunshine is a happy, joyful symbol, as most people connect sunny days with a sunny outlook.

From these symbols, you'd be pretty confident in concluding the following: the outlook for starting a family at this time is positive. The symbolism of motherhood and the eggs is especially telling, referring directly to the birth of a new situation. The color orange, representing a creative time, along with the beautiful sunshine, table setting, and flowers, all seem to indicate that this child would bring a great deal of happiness to your life. The surroundings also seem to say that the financial worries expressed about having a child at this time shouldn't be considered: everything will turn out fine. Spirit appears to be giving a clear message here that the timing is right for this and that perhaps by the springtime (indicated by the flowers) a new baby will either be present or at least expected.

As you can see from this section, dreams can be a fascinating way to become more open and receptive to messages from the spirit world. By focusing on your dreams and what happens to you during your dreamtime, you can access a whole other process for receiving spirit messages.

25   Other Exercises and Tasks

So far in this section, we've discussed symbolism and dreamwork. Now let's focus on some other exercises you can do to strengthen your connections to your spirit guides, who will in turn be better able to bring you messages from Spirit. Each of these tasks is designed to correspond directly to one of your guides in particular, and each should help you to understand how your spirit people are working in the physical world with you every day. These exercises will also prove to you how loving and helpful our spirit teachers are and how enormously happy they are to be asked to aid us anytime. These exercises are all about trusting Spirit, which is something that every medium must learn to do. Our spirit helpers are right here with us, every day. If we would only ask for their assistance when we need it! Do these exercises with a loving, open, and trusting heart, and I think you'll be amazed by Spirit's generous nature and compassionate help.

I have not included an exercise here to do with your master guide, since these higher entities are not as concerned with our everyday tasks. For now, we'll work with our joy guides, protectors, doctor teachers, and chemists and help them to help us. However, at the end of this section, you will find a meditation to do with your personal master guide that will put you in touch with an Ascended Master guide as well.

Joy Guide Exercise: Ask and You Shall Receive

More than anything, our joy guides want to see us happy. That's their job. As human beings, part of our happiness lies in our physical comfort. This exercise involves asking your joy guide to help you to achieve that in everyday life.

The next time you go to the grocery store, ask your joy guide to arrange a close parking space for you. When you're just a couple of minutes away from the store parking lot, concentrate (don't close your eyes if you're driving!) and call your joy guide to you in your mind. Ask her to get you a parking space right by the front door of the store. Focus on that thought as you drive into the parking lot. Don't be surprised if you find an empty space just waiting for you. Thank your guide, and don't be skimpy with the praise! Joy guides especially like to know they're doing a good job, so make sure you vocalize your happiness with them.

You can ask your joy guide to help you in all kinds of similar situations. Ask her to get you a table at a restaurant. To make her work a little harder, ask her to get you one quickly on a Saturday night during peak hours. Before you go to the doctor's office for your appointment, ask your joy guide to ensure that the doctor is running on time and that you won't have a long wait to see him. Ask her to prod the bank line into moving quickly before you go out on your lunch hour to cash your paycheck. Before you go online to buy your theatre tickets, ask your joy guide to arrange for excellent seats. And don't blame her if you're in the second balcony when you waited until the day before the show to try to get them. Be happy that she could get you in at all with an unobstructed view!

Whenever you try this exercise, record it and the results in your journal.

Now, the idea of this exercise is to help you feel more comfortable working with your joy guide and to prove to you that she really can help you with some very ordinary, mundane things. The object is *not* to become selfish and arrogant. Now that I know for a fact that Mara is just awaiting my call, I don't usually ask her to do these kinds of things. If it's pouring down rain when I go to the grocery store, I'll still ask for a close parking space, simply because I hate to get wet. For my wedding anniversary, I might ask her to get me a good table at a popular restaurant. Under ordinary circumstances, though, I let life be life, and I wait for my doctor, my restaurant table, and so on. Be humble and honest about your needs, and Spirit will do its best to try to help you fulfill them.

If you don't see immediate success with this exercise, keep working on it with your joy guide. Don't give up on her—or yourself.

Protector Exercise: Point Me in the Right Direction

Over the years of working with my guides, I've discovered that my protector, Arthur, is very good at helping me when I'm lost. I've driven around unfamiliar parts of town many times, disoriented and perplexed, until I've remembered to ask Arthur to help me find the store or house I'm trying to locate. When I've asked for his assistance, I invariably get a sense of which way to turn and where to go next, and eventually I end up where I'm supposed to be. I used to think I had no sense of direction. Now I realize I don't need one, because Arthur is always willing to help me out of a jam.

For this exercise, go to a shopping center or mall that's not familiar to you. When you get there, take a moment and call in your protector guide. Ask him to lead you to the nearest shoe store in the mall. When you go inside, be sure to ignore the maps of the stores, and try not to look at any indicator signs that may tell customers where to locate certain items. Rely exclusively on your guide, and follow the messages he sends to you about which way to go in the building. When you arrive at the shoe store, thank your protector guide. You can try this with other specialty stores, too, like a pet store or a frozen yogurt stand. Listen and try to recognize the signals your guide sends to you. When you're finished with your experiment, be sure to write down in your journal the kinds of signals you received. This will help to build your relationship with your protector as well as your communication with Spirit in general.

When you feel really comfortable with your protector and your communication skills, try driving to an unfamiliar location without the aid of a map. Rely only on Spirit's guidance and see how you both do. Remember to record your results in your journal, and don't forget to take your cell phone in case you need it!

Doctor Teacher Exercise: Finding Information

Since doctor teachers are wonderful to work with concerning information and study, try this exercise with yours to make your connection stronger.

Find a dictionary and sit with it on your lap. Settle yourself, close your eyes, and call to your doctor teacher in your mind. When you feel his presence, concentrate on a specific question you need answered in your life. Tell your doctor teacher that you would like an answer to this question and that you would like him to send you a message using the dictionary. Ask him to help you find the right word in the dictionary to give you some insight into your question. Hold a dictionary between your hands and continue concentrating on your doctor teacher's energy and your question. When you feel ready, keep your eyes closed but open the dictionary. Rub your hands over both pages to see which page you need to explore. Run the index finger of that hand up and down that page until you feel compelled to stop. Open your eyes. Wherever your finger has landed, read the word and definition that is printed there, and see how it fits in with the question that you asked. A word that seems strange or out of place in relation to your issue may actually fit very well once you read through all of the definitions and really meditate on the information given.

You can do this exercise with your doctor teacher anytime you need guidance on any issue. Be sure to write your questions in your journal, along with the word that your doctor teacher guides you to in the dictionary, as well as the definitions of the word and how you interpret its meaning.

I just tried this exercise again myself so that I could be sure to describe the process accurately to you as readers. I asked my doctor teacher, Dr. Wilkins, to help me understand whether or not my boys will be returning to the same school next year. This is a question that has been preying on my mind now for quite some time. At this point, my husband and I are exploring several options for them, but it looks like we will have to wait at least until the beginning of next year before we're able to decide on a course of action. I, however, am not content to wait, so I continue to question Spirit about this issue. In every other message I've received about this situation, I've basically heard the same response: "Wait and see. The outcome isn't knowable yet." Not an acceptable answer to me, as I tend to be extremely impatient. So what word did Dr. Wilkins give to me tonight as I tried this experiment with the same question?

Mystery. I just have to laugh sometimes. When will I learn?

Doctor Chemist Exercise: Tour Guide

My doctor chemist, Black Hawk, tells me that chemists are excellent teachers to work with for the following exercise. Although primarily focused on your health and well-being, chemists are also very concerned with your development as a medium, especially in how using your energy body is concerned. Try the following exercise with your doctor chemist, knowing that you are strengthening your connection to this powerful and influential spirit guide.

Think of a store or a restaurant in your area that you've never been to before. If you don't know of any, open up the yellow pages and pick a place you've never heard of. Remember the establishment's name. Next, go to your meditation space and prepare to relax. Close your eyes, center yourself, and do some deep breathing. In your mind, ask your doctor chemist to step in close to work with you on this. Feel your chemist come in, and tell her that you want to go to this place *in your mind.* Explain to your chemist that you want her to show you exactly what the place looks like inside. Then, allow your mind to open up to the images, words, sounds, smells, and everything else that your chemist brings to you concerning this visit. Be insistent: if you can't really see what the inside of the shop looks like, tell your chemist that you need to see it more clearly. Keep trying, and don't give up if you don't get anything visual. Maybe you're just being impressed with colors, music, or snippets of words. It's all important. When you feel you've received everything you're going to receive, take out your journal and write down everything you remember. Then, make a point of visiting this establishment to see how much information sent to you by your chemist coincides with reality. Be sure to keep track of how many details you can match up from her help to the real atmosphere of the place.

The first time I did this exercise, I remember seeing a lot of red, and that was about it. I've mentioned that I'm not extraordinarily clairvoyant, so I believed that seeing anything at all was beneficial. When I got a chance to visit this store in the flesh, I saw that the entire space was carpeted with a washed-out crimson shag. It was the ugliest stuff I'd ever seen, but it was beautiful to me, because I realized that Black Hawk had sent me a clear signal about the shop.

Keep a record of the times you try this exercise with your guide. The more you practice it, the better your chemist will become at being an astral tour guide and the more accurate the information you receive will be.

26   The Games
Spirit People Play

How do you feel now about working with your spirit guides? Hopefully, you feel more certain than ever of their presence, and your confidence in them is building. This is imperative to becoming a good medium, because we rely on the accuracy of the information that we receive from Spirit to make decisions for ourselves and to pass on messages to those who seek Spirit's help through us.

You should also be clearer on how you are receiving your messages from Spirit. But like everything else in life, practice makes perfect. Use the following exercises to further hone your communication skills and to have fun with your spirit guides while you're learning.

Game #1: It's All in the Cards

Use a deck of regular playing cards for this game. Take out ten cards, some in red suits and some in black suits. Don't use any face cards for this first game. Turn all the cards over so you can't see them, and make a pile. Shuffle them if you wish. Now call in your mind to your main message guide. Tell her you want to play a game.

Ask her to help you identify the cards one by one as you hold them and concentrate. She should help you to identify them as red cards or black cards only. Take the first card from the pile and hold it in your hands. Ask your guide if it's a red suit or a black suit. When you feel you've got your answer, place the card in another pile. Put red cards in the right-hand pile, and put black cards in the left-hand pile. When you've gone through all of the cards, turn your piles over and see how you did. How many did you correctly identify? Using ten cards makes it easy to arrive at a percentage. If you got six right, you scored sixty percent. That's not bad at all! Anything above sixty percent is truly outstanding. And if you didn't get many right (or none at all), don't give up. You and your guide simply need to keep working on your communication.

When you've mastered the red/black identification, try some variations on this game. Ask your guide to identify the suit (hearts, diamonds, spades, clubs) on the cards. Ask her to give you the number on the cards. Use only face cards, and ask her to identify the court member depicted on each card, including the suit. The better you and your guide get at communicating this information, the harder you need to push yourself to work. You can do this exercise anytime you feel you need more practice at communication—which, frankly, is all the time, for all of us! Keep records in your journal so you can chart your progress.

Game #2: Color My World

For this game, you'll need to visit your local home improvement store. Go and pick up several paint color swatches. Try to find the kind that only shows one block of color. If you can get ten, you'll have an easier time figuring out your percentages when you are scoring your results. Take them home, turn them over so you can't see the colors, and mix them up. Call in your message guide and tell her it's time to work again. Explain that you want her to tell you what color swatch you're holding. Pick up the first swatch in the pile, hold it in your hands, and concentrate on tuning in to your guide's message. When you feel you know, say the color out loud, and then turn the swatch over. Record in your journal whether you were right or wrong. Keep going until you've held all the swatches. How did you do?

This is another game you can play over and over again with your guide. If you're not having much luck, try asking your guide to bring you the information in a different format. Maybe she's trying to give you a picture of the color when saying the word *red* would be easier for you. Working on different methods of relaying information is often very helpful, and it's an imperative part of the learning process.

Game #3: The Name Game

For this game, you'll need some blank slips of paper. They don't have to be anything special; you can just take a piece of printer paper and cut it into ten slips. On each slip of paper, write the name of a celebrity. Try to think of people who are very diverse, people from different arenas and jobs (politics, acting, music, dance, art, sports) as well as folks who are both living and deceased. Make sure you have both male and female figures in your batch of slips. Even better: have someone else write out the slips so that you have no idea who is on them. One way or the other, try to make at least ten.

Next, sit down with your slips of paper (folded so you can't see the names, of course) and call in your guide. Tell her you are going to hold each slip of paper in turn and that right now you want to know whether the person written on the slip is male or female. That's all the information you need to try for at first. Just as with the cards, make two piles: males in the right-hand pile, females in the left-hand pile. When you're through all the slips, check your work and see how you did. Don't forget to record your results in your journal as well as write any notes about how your messages are coming through. Remember, this is just as important as the accuracy of the message.

Once you get really good at identifying male versus female names, try identifying those who have passed over versus those still alive. Then, try getting career information. Finally, try getting *all* of this for one slip of paper, including the actual name on the paper. Getting names is better if you can have someone else write up your slips, but you can't help what you know. If you know one of your slips is Marilyn Monroe and you've gotten *female, dead, actress* already, you might just make the association. This game can also be played with a partner, who can help you by saying yes or no as you try to identify your slips.

Fun and Games

As you continue working with your guides in these games, please keep in mind that they are supposed to be *fun*. They are designed to be a lighthearted way for you and your spirit people to get to know each other, to establish methods of solid communication, and to familiarize yourselves with patterns for working. They are not meant to frustrate or aggravate you. If you find yourself becoming upset when working on a game with your spirit people, *stop*. Come back to it another time. Everything in moderation. Maybe you're just trying to do too much too soon. Maybe you need to take things more slowly. Try doing only one game per day. This may seem like a very slow process, and you may not be seeing much of an improvement, but give yourself a break! Rome wasn't built in a day. Many mediums I know whom I consider to be top-notch have told me development can take years—and that's developing in a group environment, with a formal teacher. You're doing just fine. Always remember, everything is in Divine Order. You are developing at the rate at which you are meant to develop. Don't rush through the process. Sometimes the journey is much more interesting than the destination.

I won't lie to you. As I've mentioned, I'm not the most patient person on the planet, and I've been known to become very frustrated and downright angry when trying to do these kinds of games. I'm a perfectionist, too (or so I'm told), and getting anything below an eighty percent was completely unacceptable to me. As painful as these games were, I learned a lot about myself by pushing myself to keep practicing them. Ultimately, I realized that the self-knowledge was just as important as the mediumship training—perhaps even more so. We are on spiritual journeys here; there are lessons to be had in everything we do. I understand that now, and you will, too.

27 Questions? I Got Questions!

I've briefly mentioned getting answers for yourself from Spirit, but we really haven't discussed how to do that. In the doctor teacher exercise, we explored the technique of using the dictionary to get symbolic messages about pressing problems. You can certainly use this technique anytime to answer questions, but you can also use a much simpler process: call in your guide, concentrate on the issue, and ask for an answer. Does it sound easy? It should, because it really is. Let's give it a try now.

Go to your meditation space, put on your favorite music, light a candle, burn your incense—whatever you like to do to get into an open state of mind. Take some deep, cleansing breaths and feel yourself start to relax. Call to your main message guide in your mind, and tell her that you would like some insight into a problem you are having. Take as much time as you need to explain the problem in your mind. Then say, "_____ [your guide's name], please bring me clear and accurate messages that will direct me to the highest and best good concerning this issue."

Now, what's the first thing that comes into your head? Is it a sound? A flash of color? A feeling? Say it out loud: "Yellow. I see yellow." Or: "I hear the song 'Pretty Woman.'" *Whatever comes to you is the message.* Open your eyes, reach for your journal, and write it down.

What do you need to do next? Interpret the message. This is where your study of symbolism comes in. Let's say you are wondering if you should go back to school to study nursing. You've always been interested in it, but you're not sure if you'd be wasting your time or not. You're not happy in your current administrative job, but the idea of going to night school doesn't appeal to you. Then again, you feel like you need a change. Is school the right change?

So, in the first example, you saw a flash of the color yellow. Look back at your color symbolism. What does yellow mean? *Intellect, reason, mental stimulation, rational thinking.* Hmm . . . that sounds dangerously close to school and learning something new, doesn't it? From just this one symbol, it seems like your guide is acknowledging that a new course of study would benefit you.

But what about the second example? You asked about studying nursing, and you heard a snippet of the song "Pretty Woman." Now what could that possibly have to do with going back to school? Well, you may have to really think to make connections with this symbol, but I still think it can be done. To me, the song "Pretty Woman" denotes confidence and independence. It may be a message from your guide about having confidence in yourself and your abilities. Are you reluctant to go back to school because you're a little scared of the situation? Like the color yellow, I would interpret this song to be a positive message from Spirit, who seems to have faith in you. Now, in order to make positive changes in your life, you need to have faith in yourself.

If this isn't enough information for you, write down the first symbol you get, close your eyes, and ask your guide to give you more clarification. *The first thing that enters your mind is the message.* Let's say this time, you hear a bell ringing. What kind of bell is it? Is it a tinkling little bell worn by a kitten, a telephone, or an alarm? No, it's the kind of bell you used to hear in high school when it was time to change classes. *Voilà*! There's your extra message and another positive indication that going back to nursing school would be a good decision for you to make.

What if the symbols you get when you ask a question seem to be negative? For instance, using this same example, what if you saw a coffin when you asked your question? For many, a coffin symbolizes death. Some people would totally freak out to see this, because they understand death to be a terrible thing. However, most people don't realize that death itself is symbolic of a rebirth process. To see death in a message or a reading usually indicates the death of an old situation or way of life and the beginning of a new cycle. Everything dies. In the natural world, trees and other living things perish, and they usually disintegrate on the forest floor. From this detritus, this natural fertilizer, new life emerges in the spring. A new cycle begins. Our lives are no different. If I saw a death symbol in answer to this question, I would know without a doubt that Spirit was telling me that my life was changing and that letting go of old, outworn ideas and situations (including jobs) would help to usher in new, better things. The process itself (going back to school at night, continuing to work) might be challenging, but, ultimately, changing careers to become a nurse would be worth the effort.

What kinds of symbols might you receive in answer to this question if the time isn't right for nursing school? Perhaps you'd see a stop sign, signaling the need to stop and reassess your idea. Maybe you'd hear a crashing or jangling sound, which could indicate disharmony and an unwise move. You could sense anxiety wash over you immediately upon asking for guidance. All of these signals would make me think twice about the idea of this change at this time.

Don't hesitate to start asking your spirit guides for assistance with any and all issues that come up in your life. No problem is too big or too small for Spirit. All of your teachers and guides want to help you as much as possible. Allow them to do this by presenting your life circumstances to them and by opening up to the possibilities that they reveal to you. Keep track of your questions, their answers, and your interpretations in your journal. And don't forget to write it down when the outcome to the issue seems to mirror Spirit's guidance.

28   Putting It All Together

To get some more practice at interpreting symbols in the context of questions asked, take the following quiz. For each situation, choose the answer that you think is best. Write your answers in your journal, and then read through the answers I give as the best ones. See how you do on your test; more importantly, see if you can figure out *why* certain answers are better than others.

Symbol Interpretation Quiz

1. You are asked to coach your daughter's softball team. You enjoy the sport and would like to help out, but you're not sure how the extra activity will fit into your overloaded schedule. When you ask for direction, you see a fast-moving river with a canoe on it. There is a Native American in the canoe, and he is easily negotiating the waterway. How would you interpret this?

   A. Don't bother to even think about it. This is obviously a recipe for disaster.

   B. You should agree to coach. Although it may be busy, you can handle the extra obligation.

C. The Native American is probably a spirit guide, and his name could have something to do with water.

2. Your boss asks you to work on an important project with a coworker you don't like. Accepting the project would really help your performance evaluation, but you're not sure you want to deal with your coworker. When you ask for guidance, you see a rocky path going up the side of a mountain. The peak of the mountain is just barely visible through the foggy air. How would you interpret this message?

   A. The project will be a lot of hard work, and there may be some friction between you and your coworker. However, you'll eventually make it through the whole thing.

   B. The coworker won't figure into the equation at all, so make your decision based on what you feel is best for you and the company.

   C. The project will go well no matter who is involved.

3. Your mother is hospitalized with chest pains. You are naturally concerned and ask for guidance concerning her condition. When you tune in, you feel anxious and overwhelmed, but you also see a lovely blue color in your mind. How would you interpret this message?

   A. Your mother's health is in grave danger, and you need to speak to her at once about it.

   B. Your mother is stressed out and needs to take better care of herself. Healing, however, is very possible and will come to her. Showing her some meditation and relaxation techniques would really benefit her.

   C. Your mother will be out of the hospital in no time at all, and nothing further needs to be done about it.

4. Your teenage son has been staying out late, cutting class, and generally breaking the rules you've set for him. He's usually a

good kid, so you're having a hard time understanding what's going on with him. When you ask for insight, you're shown a tornado along with a chain and shackles like a convict wears in prison. How would you interpret this message?

A. Your son could have a drug problem that is turning his world upside down. You need to talk to him at once.

B. Your son is just going through a phase of rebellion, and it's OK to let him run unchecked.

C. Your son is involved with a girl, and that is overwhelming his usual sense of responsibility. He'll come around in time, probably when the relationship ends.

5. Your husband is offered a better job in another state. He can keep the one he has, thus avoiding a move, or the whole family can pack up and go. You wonder what would be the best choice for the entire family. When you tune in, you hear bright, cheerful music playing, and you see a lot of sunshine. How would you interpret these symbols?

A. Stay where you are. The grass won't be much greener in the next place.

B. The climate in the new area will be much hotter than the one you're in now. You'll probably end up with noisy neighbors.

C. The outlook for the new location looks promising for everyone involved.

All right. Let's go through each question in turn and examine the answers to see which ones are best.

In the first question, you see a Native American in a canoe, easily traveling down the river. Although this Indian could certainly be a guide, answer C is the least likely one in this case. You concentrated on a specific question (whether to coach your daughter's team), and your guides shouldn't be using that time to introduce themselves to you. Since the canoe is moving swiftly and easily through the river, and since its occupant doesn't seem to be having any trouble, the best interpretation of this symbolism is B. Coaching might make your life even busier, but it would be something that you could definitely handle. The answer in A doesn't make much sense. If the canoe were capsized in the water or if you actually saw the canoe hit a rock, then A would be a much better choice. However, since the vision is showing smooth sailing, Spirit is trying to advise you to take the coaching job.

In question #2, answer A is the best choice. Look at the symbolism in Spirit's message. A rocky, uphill climb would certainly indicate a lot of work and some possible friction between you and your coworker. The peak of the mountain barely seen is still an indication of an end in sight, even if that end is hard to reach. The other two answers don't really take the symbology given by Spirit into account.

The best answer to question #3, about your mother's health, is B. Clairsentiently, you receive the pressure in your mom's body that was caused by stress, which directly led to her heart problems. The color blue indicates that healing can and will happen but that your mom needs to address her stress level and do something about it to avoid further recurrences of this issue. Answer A is simply panicking; choice C is dismissive of the signals that Spirit has sent.

In the fourth question, you're addressing an issue concerning your teenage son and his newly rebellious actions. The shackles and chains can definitely represent confinement and restriction, so answer B, which says that he's going through a phase to break those chains, seems like a good answer. However, the tornado given in the same message indicates something much stronger and more powerful at play in this situation. Could the tornado be the girl referred to in answer C? It could be, but I am more apt to associate a tornado with a situation rather than a person. The tornado, and the chaos it creates, makes more sense to me when coupled with the shackles, which can indicate bondage to something. Drugs are an addiction; those who use them could be likened to criminals who are shackled in their cells to keep them from escaping. Because of these two powerful symbols together, I would choose A as the best answer, and I would most definitely confront my son about this new behavior.

Finally, in question #5, the sunshine and happy music indicate a brightness and lightness. Although sunshine can certainly symbolize sunny and hot weather, answer B seems almost too literal, especially in the interpretation of the music as indicating noisy neighbors. Answer A really makes no sense; how do you get a negative connotation from sunshine and happy music? This is a clear symbol that good things await the family if they choose to move. The best answer to this one is C.

So how did you do? Can you see the way in which symbols can be put together to arrive at answers to questions? Keep practicing getting your own information from Spirit, and continue working on your own symbols and their interpretations. The more you work, the more questions you ask, and the more observing you do concerning the answers that will come in time, the better medium you will grow to be.

29 Reach Out, Touch Spirit

If you page back through your journal, you should have a great record of all the progress you've made since you began your study of mediumship. Congratulate yourself on all the wonderful work you've done! You should be proud. I know you're making progress, even if it seems slow to you. Continue to work on your meditations, your exercises, and your games with your guides. All of this hard work will pay off in the end. You'll benefit physically, emotionally, and spiritually every day from your relationship with Spirit.

When you work as a medium, it is especially important to be well grounded in your own spirituality. As I mentioned in a previous chapter, it is not necessary to leave a particular religion to be a medium. You don't have to convert to Spiritualism. But it is vital to have a connection to your spirituality, no matter what it is. As long as it's positive and leads you closer to Creator, what prayers you recite, whether you worship in a church, and all of those other man-made stipulations become unnecessary and unimportant. Your relationship to God, however, is key to everything in life. Our guides, especially our master guides and the Ascended Masters of the Universe, can help us to draw closer to Creator. This is why I've been guided to share with you this Ascended Master meditation.

If you remember, Ascended Masters are beings of great enlightenment and deep spirituality. Famous names like Jesus, Buddha, and Mohammed, as well as god and goddess energies like Kuan Yin and Thoth, are included in these prestigious ranks. The Ascended Masters have great wisdom to share with all of us, and we should never feel unworthy or bothersome if we ask for their aid. They can be especially helpful in assisting us as we forge even deeper ties to Creator and to our own divine natures. Enjoy meeting with your own master guide and one of the truly inspiring Ascended Masters in this guided meditation, which focuses on deepening your spiritual connection to all things.

Master Teacher Exercise: Connecting with Ascended Masters

Prepare your surroundings and yourself for meditation. Begin by drawing deep breaths, centering, and relaxing as usual. See in your mind's eye the beautiful, bright white light of divine love pouring down over you, filling you up by entering your crown chakra, and surrounding and enveloping you in a protective egg. You are safe and at peace in the bright, protective light of Creator.

Journey to your special place. Be there instantly, and enjoy for a moment the serenity that this place brings to you. Now go to the door, knowing that your master guide awaits you on the other side of it. When you unlock the door, put away your key and open it. Your master guide is there. Greet him in whatever way feels natural to you. Behind him, see a vast firmament of stars, sparkling like diamonds upon a sheet of black velvet. You are standing on the edge of the Universe, between the many planes of existence. Your master smiles and offers his hand to you. You take it, trusting completely in him. Together, you step out into the heavens, floating weightlessly and supported effortlessly in the vast canopy of stars.

As you float with your master, you feel your body being carried along, up and up, higher and higher, into the beautiful night sky. You move at a comfortable pace, and your master's hand is tight and sure in your own. Up ahead, you can see a circle of even brighter light, one that is larger and more significant than any of the stars that surround you. You know in your soul that you are being taken to a very special place, and you feel your energy heighten. Your vibration becomes higher as you and your master draw nearer to the bright light.

Finally, you have reached it, and you and your master float into it, bathed completely in its warm, golden-white glow. Around you, you can hear music and whispers and other beautiful sounds. You feel instantly consumed by love, both for yourself and for all other living things.

You and your master slow and stop, bobbing peacefully in the beautiful white place. As you enjoy the exquisite ecstasy of your feelings, you understand that there is another presence here, one that vibrates even higher than you or your master teacher. An Ascended Master has come to this place to speak to you, and you open your heart, mind, and soul to understand who it is and what this high spiritual teacher has to share with you. Allow the presence of this Ascended Master to fill all of your spiritual senses, and know that you will understand and remember everything that happens to you in this being's presence.

(Pause for fifteen minutes.)

It is time for the Ascended Master to depart and for you to return to your own plane of existence. Thank the Ascended Master for sharing this powerful wisdom with you. Feel your consciousness begin to pull backward from the bright space as you and your master guide float back out into the starry firmament. Slowly, your master teacher takes you back to your special place, guiding you lovingly through the door and leaving you there. You are not sad, however, for you know you can meet your master teacher again anytime, simply by asking for his presence.

Now, within your special place, count backward from five to one, coming back to this reality slowly. When you get to one, you are wide awake and at peace, and you remember everything that happened to you in your meditation.

Don't forget to write down in your journal everything that happened with your master guide and the Ascended Master who visited. You can do this meditation whenever you feel that your connection to the Universe and to divinity needs to be replenished.

Part 5

READINGS
and
SITTINGS

You've been working hard over the last few weeks. You've prepared your mind and body for mediumship work by learning about the spiritual senses, the energy systems, breathing, and meditation. You've practiced meditation on a regular basis to keep your body and mind in a relaxed and open state. You've met your spirit guides and learned about why they are walking with you on your journey. You've performed exercises with your guides to help establish your methods of communication. You've learned how they may use symbolism to communicate, and you've worked with them in your dreams at night to establish an even stronger connection. You've seen how Spirit can work with you every day and how you can get answers to questions and the knowledge that you seek simply by asking for it. Hopefully, by now you feel close to at least one of your guides and are becoming more and more confident in your ability to understand spirit messages.

So are you ready now to branch out and give messages to other people?

If you're like many of my students, this idea may leave you with weak knees and a lump in your throat. It's one thing to ask Spirit to bring you answers to your own questions, because if you don't interpret the answer in the correct manner, the only person who knows about it is you. It's quite a different matter to give wrong information to another person. How embarrassing, and how awful the consequences can be, especially if the question asked was an important one.

You're quite right to be nervous about giving readings to other people. Delivering messages from Spirit carries a great deal of responsibility with it. The only way to really sharpen your mediumship skills, however, is to practice. How can you expect to keep your connection with Spirit if you don't work on it? It's fine and wonderful to get messages for yourself and to work with Spirit on your own issues, but it's terrific practice to actually bring messages to others.

In this section, we'll discuss some tips for beginning to give messages to and conduct readings and sittings for other people. Some of the information here may seem like common sense. That's because it is. Never discount practical information because it doesn't seem "spiritual" enough. We are spiritual beings having a physical experience, which means we have to adapt and live in this often rough-and-tumble world of ours. Creator gave us common sense for a reason, and it wasn't so that we could ignore it! Coupled with spiritual insight, common sense rounds us into complete people. And it never hurts us to revisit certain important topics. It simply helps them to stay fresh and active in our minds.

30   A Few Words about Divination Tools

I've been reading tarot cards for over twenty years. What started out as a fun and fascinating hobby for me turned into a spiritual journey I wouldn't trade for anything. I own many different tarot decks, and I still enjoy using tarot to gain insight into my own life as well as the lives of people who come to me for professional readings. I don't think I'll ever give up reading tarot.

If, like me, you enjoy using a divination tool, there isn't any reason you can't incorporate that tool into your mediumship readings. Runes, I Ching, tarot, playing cards, oracle cards, scrying—all of these can easily contribute to a mediumship reading. The task is to figure out the best way to incorporate the tool into the reading. Will you start by throwing out cards and reading those, veering off from your visual aid when Spirit gives you something important to say? Will you allow your sitter to ask questions and then cast your runes to answer them? Will you start by giving your mediumship reading and then ask the sitter to pose any questions she might have, using your oracle to guide you? There are myriad ways to conduct the reading itself, and it's a completely individual choice for every reader. But if you want to use a divination tool, do. It may make your reading that much better.

Before you use your tool in a reading, be sure to bless it and to ask for Spirit to use it well during your readings. Try a blessing like this one:

Divination Tool Blessing

Take your divination tool to your meditation space. Light candles and incense if you like, and play relaxing music to set a reverent mood. When you have taken several deep breaths to center your-self, hold your divination tool in your hands. Press the tool between the palms of your hands as you close your eyes and see the beautiful bright white light of the Universe surrounding it. This energy is positive and filled with blessings. As you continue to visualize the white light, call in your spirit guides. Feel them gather close, forming a circle that surrounds you with even higher and more positive energy. Watch the white light around your divination tool envelop you and your circle of spirit friends. In this light, you feel safe, calm, and peaceful. Nothing but good can come to you, and nothing but good can go from you. Continue holding your tool, and say:

> I ask for Creator's blessing upon this _____ [tarot deck, crystal ball, or other tool]. I ask that it only be used for positive purposes and that it be a clear and precise channel for spirit communication. I ask all of my guides and teachers in Spirit to use this _____ [tarot deck, crystal ball, or other tool] as a reliable method of communication. I ask that the messages I receive through this tool be accurate, correct, and for everyone's highest and best good. In the holiest name, I pray. Amen.

When you are finished with your prayer, take your tool and put it in a place of honor on your altar or in your meditation space.

Remember too that if you choose to use a divination tool, you will need to clean it energetically at least once a month. All divination tools pick up negative energies from those who come for readings. I usually try to remember to clear my tarot cards during the waning moon phase, the perfect time to release unwanted energies. You can find the waning moon on any calendar that prints the moon cycles. When the moon is waning, or getting smaller, the energies of the Universe are best for cleansing and releasing. To clear a tool of negative energies, you can bathe it in sea salt. This will wipe away all dark energy that has accumulated on the tool. Since you can't soak tarot or oracle cards in water, I suggest putting them on a tray or in a basket and setting them outside in bright sunshine or on a night when the waning moon is especially visible. Leave them out for at least a half an hour, and these natural spotlights will dissipate any negative energies your cards have accumulated.

Now we're ready to give a reading to someone else. But who to ask?

31 The Victim

I'm joking when I call our sitter "the victim," you know. In all honesty, however, when you're first starting out giving messages to others, the person whom you read for is going to be the proverbial guinea pig. As long as you both know this going into the reading, everyone should be in good shape. And at this point, of course, you aren't charging money for readings. You're doing this to practice your skills and to learn more and more about how Spirit brings messages to you for others. But let's get back to our original question: who do we ask to sit with us as we struggle through this new process?

Start with your family or close friends. By now, if you live with someone, she probably has an inkling that you're interested in "this mediumship stuff." More than likely, she's seen this book lying around, and maybe the two of you have even discussed some of what you've read. Ask her to sit down with you during a quiet time of the day so that you can tune in and see if Spirit has anything to say to her.

If you live alone or if you don't feel comfortable asking someone with whom you share accommodations, approach a friend. Asking a close friend makes it a little easier for you both, because it's important that each of you feels comfortable with the process. Make a time when you can get together in a quiet setting so that you can see what Spirit brings through for him.

What if you have people around you who are not very open to the idea of Spirit contact? What if your entire family and your friends don't believe in after-death communication and deride you for your interest in this subject? Well, this certainly makes practicing your new skills harder, but it doesn't make it impossible! Perhaps someone whom you work with is open minded and would be interested in receiving a reading. If you don't want to tell business associates about your new studies, you can find interested parties through chat rooms and e-mail lists on the Internet. If you don't have access to a computer at home, go to the library and log on. I know for a fact that there are many groups at places like http://groups.yahoo .com that discuss esoteric and spiritual subjects. These groups will list their interests and topics on the main page, and you can choose groups that seem to fit what you're looking for. Once you join a group, lurk for a bit to get an idea about the energy of the participants before you post any messages. See if people seem open to the idea of readings. Some groups may even encourage their members to give each other messages. When you feel at home, jump into the conversations and politely tell other users that you are studying mediumship and could use some practice. You may be able to do a reading for another list member through e-mail, a chat room, or an instant-messaging service. This will be very different energetically from giving someone a reading in person, but you and your guides can handle it by working together. And you may be pleasantly surprised at what great information comes through.

Of course, you need to be careful in cyberspace, and you need to exercise (say it with me again!) common sense. Don't use your real name in a chat room. Make up a pseudonym so that people can't track you. Never give out personal information in a chat room or on a group e-mail list. There is no reason any of these folks need to know your name, mailing address (different from your e-mail address!), or telephone number, and they certainly don't need to know your social security number or anything about your checking account! If they ask you for this type of information, *leave immediately* and report the group or list to the website administrator. Discernment goes a long way on the Internet, just as it does when working with Spirit. And please don't forget your spirit helpers if you decide to give the web a whirl. If you ask them to help, they'll lead you to the perfect group of people to fit your needs. Believe me, I know. I've met some truly great friends through the Internet.

Now that you've found someone who wants to contact Spirit, let's discuss how to conduct a reading or sitting. For the record, a *sitting* is an old-fashioned Spiritualist term for communing with Spirit. In my training, we called it "sitting for Spirit," which included meditating and working with our own spirit guides as well as sitting with another person to channel messages to them from their spirit loved ones. But no matter what you call it, the following chapters contain some practical guidelines I've learned over the past twenty years for giving a successful reading.

32   Introductions

Obviously, when you're first starting out, you'll most likely be working with people who you know. This is actually a good thing, because, like I said before, it will make both you and the person receiving the reading more comfortable. Believe it or not, some folks are actually nervous when they come for a reading. I've found that this is mostly due to the negative stereotypes that the media, religious institutions, and other sources have perpetuated about contacting the spirit world. A lot of people have been brought up in faith systems that frown upon or even forbid this type of work. When they come for a reading, they are anxious that a "punishment" is forthcoming for them, and I think they subconsciously anticipate hearing bad news in a reading. I've even had people tell me, "I want to get a reading, but I don't want to hear anything bad." Well, gee, neither do I! What do we as mediums do in situations like these?

First, I think it's important to address the person's fear issues. If they are afraid because of their belief system, assure them you are doing nothing that in any way undermines the teachings in the Bible and other sacred texts. Many Christian denominations get upset about the idea of mediumship and after-death communication. Spiritualists believe that Jesus himself was a medium because he was able to communicate with spirit entities (Elijah, Moses, the angels), he was able to heal people of terrible diseases and conditions, and he was able to prophesize. To Spiritualists, Jesus was the greatest medium ever. Many Christians balk at this label, however, because it disturbs their belief in Jesus as savior. Whether you believe in Jesus as savior or not is irrelevant; the bottom line is that Jesus himself told us that all of the things he did (the healing, the prophecy, the spirit communication) could be done by us as well. In the gospel of John 14:12, Jesus says, "I am telling you the truth: those who believe in me will do what I do—yes, they will do even greater things, because I am going to the Father" (*Good News Bible*). Well, I believe in Jesus—not in the Christian sense of Jesus as savior, but in Jesus as Christ, that he achieved the Christ Consciousness, the attainable higher state of consciousness that brings us closer and closer to divinity until we are one with it. And here, in this Bible passage, Jesus says, "Hey, you know all those wonderful miracles I performed? Well, you can do them, too, if you believe in yourself and your own divinity, just like I believe in my own divinity." To me, it is wrong to criticize mediums and preach that communicating with Spirit is evil. Jesus did it, and he wasn't evil. I'm not evil, either, and neither is the process of communicating with Spirit.

The fear that people have of receiving bad news in a reading is also one you can address when you first sit down with your client. This is a golden opportunity to talk to your client about personal responsibility and the way our perceptions color our world. Personally, I don't believe anything negative will come through in any reading, but that's *my* perception of things. I don't see many situations as negative ones; I prefer to think of them as *challenges*. We all encounter obstacles in our lives: we lose our jobs; we go bankrupt; we endure a nasty divorce or the breakup of a relationship; our friends or family members pass away. Are these painful, sometimes heartbreaking situations? Yes, of course they are, and I'm not trying to minimize their significance in any way. Our perception of them, however, can make them easier or more difficult to deal with. Sometimes Spirit gives us a "heads up" about a coming situation so we can better prepare ourselves to handle it. If my business is going to close, I think I'd rather know about it in advance than have it blindside me when it actually occurs. If I know it's going to happen, I have the opportunity to sock away some extra money and to type up a resume so that I'm ready when the doors shut and the income stops. I can also begin manifesting another employment opportunity for myself by doing some helpful affirmations, through prayer and ritual, and by beginning a job search. Throughout this process, I keep a positive attitude, knowing that all is in Divine Order and that these changes are happening because I need them to occur in my life. Isn't this a more productive way of looking at this situation than wallowing in despair over the job loss? If you can help your clients to see negative situations as challenges to be met and overcome, they will be much better equipped to handle anything that comes to them. They'll also be less fearful of the process of communicating with Spirit.

When I begin a reading, I always start by telling my client what to expect during the session. I like to describe to her what I will be doing in the reading and how the communication process works. I've found that a lot of people are not familiar at all with what mediumship really is and what I have to do as a medium to bring through messages from Spirit. Again, this is a great opportunity to educate people. I find that it is helpful to explain to the sitter how I receive messages and how those symbols, words, and feelings may be interpreted during the reading. I also tell people that no medium can guarantee who is going to come through from the spirit world to deliver messages. Many folks come to a reading hoping to hear from a particular person who has passed away. Having this expectation is fine, but it's also important to understand that sometimes certain spirits may not come through for a variety of reasons and that the medium cannot control that.

Remember the first rule of mediumship? *You control Spirit.* This might seem to be a contradiction, but it's not. Just because our loved ones have passed into spirit does not mean they have lost the gift of free will. Sometimes, our loved ones don't come through because they choose not to at that time. Maybe they don't know they *can* communicate. Some spirits don't realize that they have the power to communicate with those still in the physical world. Some may have recently made their transition to Spirit or may still be acclimating themselves to the spirit world, and they may be unable to communicate for these reasons. Others may just be too busy at that particular time to come through. I like to tell my clients that our loved ones aren't over there just sitting on a cloud and playing a harp. They are continuing to learn and grow in the spirit world, and they may be otherwise occupied with something important when someone from the physical plane wishes to talk with them. When a beloved family member or friend doesn't come through in a reading, it's not because we are unimportant. As a medium, it's imperative that you help your clients to understand this, preferably before you begin a reading for them. This way, they're more likely to be satisfied with the reading they receive, and if the person actually does come through to speak, it's an added bonus to their experience.

If you use an additional divination tool when you perform your readings, it's a good idea to mention that before the session with your client begins. Some folks only want to talk to Spirit in a reading, and they will not understand why you need to use runes or tarot cards to help you make a connection with the spirit world. If you do need these tools, it's only fair to explain to the client beforehand what they are and how you intend to use them. Having been a tarot reader for twenty years and a medium for eight, I have a mixture of clients who see me for readings. I still occasionally use tarot or oracle cards during a reading, if Spirit prompts me to do so. I always tell my clients up front that I may or may not use the cards, depending on what Spirit inspires me to do. Some clients will enjoy having another divination tool accessed during their reading; some clients will see it as a waste of time and only want to hear directly from Spirit. How you decide to conduct your readings is completely up to you. Just make sure that you explain your process to your clients before you begin.

The last thing I recommend doing before beginning a reading is saying a prayer. The positive energy of prayer helps to center you as the medium, and it helps the client become more focused and relaxed. Most people will respond well to the idea of a prayer, especially if you explain to them that it helps you to get into their vibration and that it sets up a positive and productive energy around the reading situation. Even if the person for whom you are reading is not a religious person, he will most likely respect your need for centering and won't object to a prayer. Some mediums prefer old standard prayers, like the "Our Father" from Christian tradition or the 23rd Psalm from the Bible. If you'd like something more non-denominational, you can certainly write one of your own. Here is a prayer I've been saying before readings and circles for years. I've changed some of the words to suit myself, and I am not even sure where this prayer originated. Nonetheless, it helps me to get right into the proper frame of mind for a reading, and it lets my spirit guides know that it's time to work.

Dear Mother-Father God, we ask Thy blessing upon us as we sit together. We pray for wisdom, and we pray for understanding. Send Thy ministering spirits unto us to reveal to us the truth; to help us to live our lives in such a way as to fulfill the karma of this incarnation; to help us attain happiness, health, peace, and prosperity; to be of service to You, and to others. Amen.

Once I've said that prayer, my spirit people are ready to work, and so am I. Let's talk now about the actual reading part of a session and how to handle some situations that may arise.

33   The Messages

Begin a reading with a client by doing exactly what you've been practicing all along: give the first thing that comes into your mind. Say it out loud: "I'm seeing a stone wall for you." Now comes your first challenge in the reading: what does the stone wall mean? It could be a literal stone wall that surrounds an actual piece of property, or it could be a symbolic stone wall, which will need interpretation. How do you know which it is? *Ask your guide.* In your mind, ask for some clarity about whether the wall is figurative or literal, and you should feel a sense one way or the other. If you don't, *keep asking until you get an answer.* This is how your guide learns what kind of information you need in a reading and how she needs to send it to you. It's all right to tell your client that you need a moment. You're practicing, remember? Heck, I'm a professional, and I still say to my clients, "Hold on a minute," when I'm trying to clarify information as it's coming through in a reading. You want to make sure what you're getting is clear and accurate, right? This is one way to do that.

Once you feel you have a handle on the message, go ahead and elaborate on it: "I feel that this stone wall is symbolic." Great! You've determined that the person doesn't own property surrounded by a stone wall and that Spirit is instead trying to convey an idea to the sitter by using this imagery. That means it's up to you now to interpret the symbol. What does the stone wall mean? If you are seeing it clairvoyantly, look at the details of the wall. Is it in good repair, or is it falling apart? Is it overgrown by weeds? Is the grass next to it high or the trees around it mature? Is it raining? All of these are clues and can add meaning to the message. Yes, you've got a lot of work to do to sort it all out. Let's take each example one at a time so you can see how a message can grow out of one simple image.

If the stone wall is in good repair, it probably represents a wall around something in your client's life. Why do we build walls? To keep things out. Perhaps your client has built a wall around himself as a protective measure. If the wall is in good repair, he's done an excellent job of it. Or maybe Spirit is trying to tell him that he's built such a strong wall around himself that he's not allowing anyone in. See how you feel when you are looking at the wall. Do you feel relaxed, or does it make you feel sad or nervous? These are indications from Spirit about whether the wall is a good idea or a bad one.

What about a wall that's falling apart? If your sitter built the wall as a protective device, it's time to repair it. Otherwise, it looks like the wall is crumbling as the sitter moves forward, which can be an encouraging thing. Spirit could be congratulating the client on making progress in tearing down walls. The sitter could be in the process of overcoming an obstacle in his life. Again, see how you feel when looking at the scene to get a better handle on this part of the interpretation.

If the wall is overgrown by weeds, it could mean that something bothersome is overtaking his progress. If the wall is an impediment already, the weeds could represent a further restriction that he will have to deal with. However, all he has to do is a little gardening and he'll be able to get back on track.

If the wall is surrounded by lots of foliage, the client has great potential for growth, and this one small obstacle (the wall) is really the only thing standing between him and success. Encouraging him to face his wall head-on and without fear can only help him.

Rain in a message like this one could represent a need for cleansing, for tearing down a wall in the emotional realm. Perhaps by examining his feelings and concentrating on his inner landscape, the client can break through any existing walls he's created, enabling him to live a happier and more productive life.

Wow! All of that out of one little symbol! Can you see how you can take something as simple as a wall and turn it into a powerful message?

Now, what if the wall wasn't symbolic? What if you feel the wall is literally something that surrounds the sitter's property? Well, the only way to know for sure is to say, "I feel like this is an actual wall on an actual piece of property. Do you own a piece of land surrounded by a stone wall?" If he says yes, terrific! Spirit has given you something *evidential,* meaning a piece of information that the client can verify is accurate. Sometimes Spirit will do this just to affirm that you are in the right vibration and nothing more. On the other hand, Spirit may bring something like this through if you are supposed to talk about the thing itself. Ask your guide if there is further information to go along with this wall. Maybe you'll be shown something that indicates an increase in property or, on the other hand, the idea of selling the property. Keep asking for more information from your guide until you feel the information has come through completely.

If your sitter says no, he doesn't own a piece of property with a wall, then *ask your guide for clarification.* Maybe he's going to visit a place like the one you're seeing and it's going to be a very significant trip. Maybe he's going to purchase a place like this sometime and Spirit is telling him about it because it will also be significant.

Or maybe (horror of horrors!) you interpreted the message wrong. It happens. Maybe it's supposed to be a symbol, and you felt it was literal. Oops! Now wait for a second and answer me this:

Did the world stop?

Of course it didn't. You're going to make mistakes when you read for other people. You probably made mistakes while doing your exercises and playing games with your guides, right? This is no different, so don't be hard on yourself. Never forget: the wall *is* the message. You're getting that blasted wall for a reason, and it's coming from Spirit. Go ahead and interpret it symbolically for the person, and keep asking your guide to bring you more and more clarity as you work.

34   Look Who's Talking

One of the most important components of a mediumship reading, rather than a regular psychic reading, is the presence of Spirit. This means it is imperative in a mediumship reading to identify for the sitter who it is who is coming through to talk. I'm sure you're working with your gatekeeper to get messages. It's important to know, however, who is talking to your gatekeeper on the Other Side. Most people are anxious to get a mediumship reading because they want to hear from their loved ones in Summerland. As mediums, we need to make sure we don't forget this vital part of our readings.

Let's go back to our example. You sat down with your client, and you saw a stone wall. You felt it was symbolic and interpreted it as such for the sitter. He was excited to receive what he felt to be an important and meaningful message. Now you need to tell him who brought the message to him. How do you determine this? *Ask your guide.* She's standing right there with the sitter's spirit friend on the Other Side, and she can tell you who is speaking.

What kind of information might you receive in answer to this request? Maybe you'll hear a name: "James." If this is the case, say to your client, "I am hearing the name James. Do you understand that name?" At this point, you don't know if James is the one on the

Other Side speaking or if the spirit person is calling out the name of someone he knows here in the physical world (that is, someone who's still alive). Ask your guide again for clarification. Maybe you'll see a young man and get a strong impression that he's passed into spirit. Say to the client, "I feel that James has passed over and was younger when he passed. Do you understand?" Always give what you get. You never know when something you might think is silly or stupid makes a meaningful and deep connection for someone grieving the loss of a loved one.

Hopefully, if you get a name, the sitter will recognize the spirit easily. "Oh, yes, I know a James who has passed," he might say. Wonderful! But if your sitter doesn't understand the name, acknowledge it and *keep going*. "Well, I'm hearing the name James. Please remember that, because it might make sense later on. It could be someone either here in the physical world or someone who's passed." You wouldn't believe the number of people who come to a mediumship reading and don't remember the names of all of the people they know who've made their transition to the Other Side. I've even done it myself, forgetting for years that I had a younger cousin who died named Theresa. I would have mediums get the name Theresa around me, but I couldn't figure out why. My poor cousin had been trying to get my attention for some time before I finally realized that I *did* have a Theresa in Summerland!

You may be able to identify a spirit coming through by an impression or feeling of who they are. Maybe you just need to say the word *father*. So say it to your client: "I keep wanting to talk about a father to you. I feel your father is in Spirit. Do you understand?" If you get a yes, great! If not, *keep going, keep working*. Your guides are doing the very best they can, and so are you. Don't forget about in-laws and stepfamily connections, too. My father-in-law is in Spirit, and he sometimes comes through to mediums with a father vibration. I can't fault a medium for that; on the Other Side, fathers, fathers-in-law, and stepfathers may all be lumped together. It could also be someone who was *like* a father to your sitter. Sometimes these ties can be very hard to sort out, but hang in there. It'll become clearer the more you work with your guides.

Another way to identify who is coming through in a reading is to describe them, if you are able to see them clairvoyantly. Perhaps you say to your sitter, "I see a man with silver and brown hair, parted on the side. He's wearing a shirt and trousers underneath a long apron. Do you understand who this is?" The sitter says, "Oh, yes, that's my father. He was a butcher."

Remember too that the person delivering a message from the Other Side might be the client's own spirit guide. Many people aren't aware that they have spirit guides, and they'll be interested to know who their guides are and what their guides have to say. If you see, sense, or hear a guide, be sure to pass that information along to your client. You can also pass on the knowledge that you have learned about spirit guides and how to work with them. Maybe this is a big message for your sitter, and he'll certainly benefit from his relationship with his spirit guides no matter what else you get in the reading.

Once you've identified those two components—*who* is delivering a message and *what* the message from Spirit is—you've successfully given your first mediumship message to another person. Excellent job! Now your reading continues on from there in the same vein. Maybe you'll get another impression about someone new coming in from Spirit to speak. Identify them and then see what message they are bringing with them. Give these to your sitter, and pretty soon you'll be fifteen minutes or a half an hour into a reading.

You can also allow your sitter to ask questions during his reading. Simply say, "Do you have any questions?" If he asks something, hold the question in your mind and ask your spirit guides and his spirit people to give you a clear answer to it. Again, you may see a symbol, you may hear a word, or you may get an impression of how to answer. Give what you get, and do your best to interpret the symbols as you see them.

35   The Don't List

As you become more proficient at giving messages to friends and doing readings for others, you may have people who ask you to read for them. This is great practice, but keep in mind a few things:

- Don't read if you feel overly tired or ill. This can negatively affect your ability to concentrate and to accurately deliver messages from Spirit. Wait until you feel better.

- Don't read if you or your sitter have ingested alcohol or illegal drugs. These substances can impair your ability to receive messages accurately, and they can also open you up too much to the spirit realms. Remember the Law of Attraction: *like attracts like.* Using drugs or alcohol before tuning in to the spirit world can allow lower, negative entities and energies to attach themselves to you. Don't jeopardize yourself in this way.

- Don't read anywhere that you feel uncomfortable. At first, it may be wise to read only in your own home, in a space that feels good to you. If your meditation/prayer space is large enough, it's an excellent place to conduct a reading. Dining rooms work well, too, because the table is nice for displaying special objects, candles, incense, or a divination tool that you need to access. Be sure to take the phone off the hook, put the dog out in the yard, and get rid of any other distractions that might interrupt your reading. If you have small children, it is never a good idea to read with them around unless you have a nanny or babysitter who can keep an eye on them. If you feel comfortable reading at a friend's house, go ahead, but be sure to honor your feelings and instincts. If you feel nervous and edgy in a particular room in your friend's house, don't read there. You're picking up negative vibrations, and you need to listen to your intuition. At this point, don't read in a noisy environment, like a bar or a party. Somewhere down the road, you may feel more confident about conducting readings at parties or for large groups of people, but for now, stick to a quieter, less stressful place.

- Don't read for more than one person at a time. Some folks may try to talk you into doing a "couple reading," or they may say they feel more comfortable letting their best friend sit in while you read for them. I would advise against this. When you are first beginning, it is hard enough identifying spirit people and delivering their messages to just one person. Two people will have different spirit energies wishing to speak to them, and it can become very confusing for a medium to try to determine which spirit being wants to communicate with whom. Give yourself a break and only read for one person at a time. When you feel more confident of your abilities, it will be easier for you to distinguish between spirit energies, their messages, and the objects of their attention in the physical world.

- Don't read for someone too often. Some people have a tendency to become what I like to call "spirit junkies." They come to a point where they feel compelled to consult their spirit guides about what color to dye their hair or what pillows to buy to match their couch. This is *not* what Spirit wants for us. Our spirit people are more than happy to help us make important decisions, but they do not want to usurp our free will. If you've given a long (twenty to thirty minutes) reading to a friend in the last month, she probably doesn't need one for at least another six weeks, unless the circumstances in her life have changed drastically (such as she lost her job or had an unexpected pregnancy). Spirit probably won't have much new to say anyway!

- Don't dispense medical advice under any circumstances. If a person needs medical information or guidance, Spirit is *not* the place to get it. He needs to see a doctor, chiropractor, or someone else with medical training. You must be very careful when talking about health issues in a reading. If you sense that a person is in need of a professional medical opinion, say something like, "I feel Spirit is trying to get you to see a doctor. I would take this advice if I were you, as soon as possible." Upon hearing this, many clients will try to get you to tell them what's wrong. Don't, even if you feel you know for sure. The problem is that anything you say can be misconstrued as medical advice, which can leave you wide open for legal recourse somewhere down the road. You need to protect yourself. Just telling the client that Spirit is concerned about his health should be enough. You have given the message and, like all other messages, it is up to the sitter to take that information and act on it as he sees fit.

- Don't read for someone who is setting you up for failure. You know the type. She just says no to everything you tell her. If you've read for her before and she negated every piece of information Spirit brought to her, why put yourself through that again? More than likely, she didn't *want* to hear what Spirit had to say. You need to protect your energy, too. Politely tell her that you don't feel your last reading went very well and that you'd prefer not to read for her again. Recommend that she learn to trust her own intuition and spirit helpers so that she can solve her problems on her own, or refer her to someone else who does readings.

- Don't give up if you have "bad" readings. We all have days when we're off, just like everyone else. Perhaps a reading doesn't go well simply because you're having *that* kind of a day. If you are getting a constant stream of "no" answers from your client (and she doesn't fall into the category discussed above), maybe you're having an off day. Tell your sitter you're sorry, but maybe it'd be better if you read for her another time. Perhaps some time spent in meditation and relaxation with your guides would be helpful. And remember, you're still new at all this. Be easy on yourself! You're allowed to make mistakes. Keep in mind, too, that no reader can be the be-all and end-all of mediums. There may be people with whom your energies simply don't mesh. In other words, you might not be able to deliver good readings for every person you sit with. It happens. Every now and again, I'll encounter a person for whom I can get nothing but garbage. Now that I've been at this for a while, I can usually recognize these people instantly, as soon as I sit down with them. I get a sort of static feeling in my head, like a radio that's not tuned right. I'll try for a couple of minutes to see if I can clear it out, but usually I'll end up saying, "I'm sorry, I'm simply not getting anything for you. I feel like I might not be the right person for you to see for a reading. Let me give you the name and phone number of someone I think is an excellent medium."

- Don't give up! Your spirit guides want to work with you. Keep doing your meditations, your exercises, and your games, and you *will* become more proficient at spirit contact. It may take a while, but it's worth it. As my eighth-grade teacher always used to say, "Excellence is always worth the effort."

36   Some Tips about Evidence

When reading for other people and bringing through their loved ones in the spirit world, you may find that your sitter is very interested in what mediums call *evidential messages*. These are, as described earlier, tidbits of information that the loved one in Spirit will give to the medium that prove to the sitter beyond a doubt that he or she really is speaking from beyond the grave. As a medium-in-training at Camp Chesterfield, I learned that one of the most important tasks of a Spiritualist medium is to prove the continuity of life, that is, that we continue on after we die and that death is not the end of existence. One way to prove this to the people left behind in the physical world is to give them unquestionable information that they would recognize. And this is one of the hardest things to do as a medium.

One reason evidential information is difficult is simply because the people in Spirit still have free will. As much as we as mediums control Spirit (meaning that we can organize them in our readings, keep away spirits we don't wish to speak to, and so on), we cannot control the information that comes through in a reading. A sitter who is anxious to hear from her deceased father about the will he left behind might become very upset if her father does indeed come through but mentions nothing about the estate she so desperately wishes to discuss. Is this the medium's fault? No, it isn't. It really isn't Spirit's fault, either. Usually, our spirit loved ones have moved beyond all of these earthly concerns. They simply want us to know that they see us and they love us, and they want us to be aware of their continued existence. A sitter should really come to a reading with no expectations whatsoever and be open to whatever Spirit has to bring to him; this scenario, however, is very rare. When we mourn for someone who has passed and long for them to be with us again, we are not always reasonable about the contact we want to receive. This is human nature, after all. When my mother passed away, I wanted her to come through *immediately,* and I can remember railing at her and at my guides for not bringing her through posthaste. I'm human, too, even though I understand how Spirit works. Again, this is where explaining some of this to your client in the introduction part of your reading will help.

However, getting a piece of evidence for your sitter is something you should strive for in your readings. When you first begin, try for one piece of good, solid evidence concerning Spirit and who is speaking to your sitter. This could be a name, a relationship to the sitter, a description of the spirit speaking, or some detail from the spirit loved one's life that the sitter could identify.

Let's go back to our previous example with the stone wall. You give the symbol and interpret it. Then, you ask your spirit guide to tell you who is bringing the message to the sitter. You feel that you need to say the word *father,* and so you say to your client, "I am receiving an impression of a father vibration. Has your father passed away?" The client affirms that yes, his father has passed. Now, to confirm even further that this truly is your sitter's father communicating from Spirit, you say to your guide, "Give me something else to prove this is his father." Wait and see what comes in. Perhaps you'll hear a name or even see a letter of the alphabet. When you state the name, your client confirms this is his father's name. If it's just a letter, say, "I see the letter *J,* and I feel it's connected to your dad. Did his name begin with the letter *J*?" Your sitter confirms for you that yes, his father's name was John. Excellent! Now you have your proof that you are truly connected to your sitter's father.

Maybe instead of a name, you feel a sensation of pressure in your chest. Often, sensations like this are connected to physical conditions that the spirit person had while still in the body. They can also be indications of how the person passed into spirit. If you're having trouble breathing, you might say, "I feel a restriction in my chest that's connected to your dad. Did he have a breathing condition?" Your sitter confirms that yes, his father suffered from emphysema. Great! You've gotten a good piece of evidence for your sitter.

Perhaps you see something in your mind that is connected to this spirit, such as an open field of wheat waving in the sunshine. In the background, you notice a tractor along with a house and barn way off in the distance. You say, "I am seeing what looks to me like a farm. Did your father have any connections to a farm?" Your sitter nods and replies, "Yes, my father grew up on a farm in Iowa." Wonderful job! You've gotten the evidence you need to confirm that this is the sitter's dad.

But what happens if your sitter can accept nothing that you tell him as evidence? Go back to the first example, with the letter *J*. When you ask about it, your client says, "No, my father's first name was Harold." That's not a letter *J*, is it? What about his last name? Never discount surnames as evidence. If the father's last name isn't the *J*, then perhaps there is someone in the physical world whom the sitter's father is trying to acknowledge whose name begins with *J*. Maybe he had a close friend whose name begins with *J*. If your sitter still can't relate to this *J* name, then let it go by saying, "Well, this is what Spirit is showing to me. Just remember it, and it may make more sense later on." Now what do you do?

You keep working, and you keep pushing your guide to do her job! Ask your guide for a piece of information from the sitter's father that the sitter will easily connect to his dad. You can even ask specific questions: What did his dad do for a living? How many years ago did his dad pass away? In which month was his birthday? How many brothers and sisters did he have? How did he make his transition? These are all questions that you should be able to get answers to that can give you the piece of evidence you need to prove that you are communicating with the sitter's deceased father.

Remember, be easy on yourself. Evidence is *hard*. Not only are you asking for something very specific from Spirit, but you are putting yourself on the line with another person when you tell him what you get as a response. *You will probably be wrong some of the time,* especially when you are first beginning. This is all part of the learning process. You might become frustrated with your spirit guides, but try to understand that they are doing the best they can, just as you are. You are learning together, and eventually your communication skills will improve. Keep trusting in the process, and you'll start to get better and more accurate information.

37 Broaching the Subject of Death

Every person deals differently with pain and loss. When you conduct mediumship readings, you are doing so with the intention that people who have passed into spirit will communicate with you and your client. These people may have died twenty years ago or two days ago. The client who is sitting with you could be delighted by a spirit's presence, or he could be devastated all over again as he relives the loss of his loved one. As a medium, it is imperative that you be sensitive to these emotions.

When I am conducting a reading and a sitter begins to cry when a loved one steps in, I offer the client some tissues and ask, "Would you like me to continue?" Usually, the sitter indicates that she wants the reading to go on. Occasionally, the presence of the passed loved one is too overwhelming for the sitter, and we end the session. You must honor whatever it is that your client wants. After all, it's her loved one and her reading. If she does opt to discontinue the reading, offer to read for her at a later time, when she may be feeling more in control of her emotions. Be sympathetic and supportive of her until she feels ready to leave.

The way a person made his transition can also be a sensitive subject in a reading. Use gentle tact if you need to describe a person's death. This information can be very evidential, but it's important to realize that this can cause pain for your client. It may be wise to ask your sitter if he would like this information: "I feel like your dad is trying to tell me about the circumstances surrounding his death. Shall I continue?" This way, you've asked your sitter permission to give him this evidence, and you've provided him an opening to refuse this information if he feels it's too much for him. If he'd like you to go on, be as compassionate as you can be when describing a passing: "Your dad is showing me a hospital room, and I can hear the beeping of a heart monitor. I feel he passed very slowly after a long illness. Is this right?" Once your sitter confirms this for you, you can move on to the message his father is trying to highlight.

Be especially careful in readings when you feel suicide or murder was involved. These two situations can be excruciatingly painful for those left behind, and heavy feelings of guilt, shame, and even anger can engulf the client when these issues are addressed. Even the way you word this in a reading can help to soften the blow of hearing about it again. I will usually say to my clients, "I don't want to bring up a painful situation, but this man is telling me he caused his own death. Did he take his own life?" This is much more compassionate than saying, "I see that he committed suicide."

In the instance of a murder, remember that it is not your job, or Spirit's, to solve a criminal case. This loved one may simply want the fact that he was murdered acknowledged; more than likely, he will leave the investigative activities up to the authorities. However, if something does come through that seems to be connected to the murder, don't hesitate to give the information to your client. Just be especially gentle in the way you handle this kind of verification from Spirit.

38   Ending a Reading

The best way to end a reading is to be honest with your sitter: "That's all I have to give to you today." You will know when the spirits have pulled back. The energies will be harder to access. You may even feel drained or tired. When this happens, it's best to stop. If you push yourself and your spirit people to get more information, you'll be working twice as hard and you'll probably end up exhausting yourself, not to mention the fact that you might not get very good information from Spirit. Be sure to thank your client for allowing you to serve, and be sure to thank your guides, too, for helping you.

How can you measure the success of a reading? One way is to ask your client what he thought and if he is satisfied with the results. Since you are learning, this type of feedback is the only way you're going to know how well you did as a medium. Be open to any comments your sitter may give to you. Everything should be helpful to you in some way. Try to get details from your client about what he liked or didn't like about the reading. An easy way to get feedback is to use a written evaluation form. This may sound like a lot of work, but it's really very simple. Use the example here, photocopy it, and politely ask your clients to fill it out. People will tend to be much more honest when they are writing a critique. Encourage them to be as forthright as they can be. An evaluation can only help you to know where you need to focus your efforts in your meditations and work with your guides.

Reading Evaluation Form

1. Had you ever received a reading before? What type of reading had you received?

2. Did I explain my reading process to you in enough detail?

3. Did I make you feel at ease during the reading?

4. Please rate how well I explained the information received during the reading to you:

Excellent	Good	Satisfactory	Needs Improvement	Poor
1	2	3	4	5

5. Please rate how well I answered the questions you posed in your reading:

Excellent	Good	Satisfactory	Needs Improvement	Poor
1	2	3	4	5

6. Did you receive proof in your reading, that is, names of passed loved ones, dates, or information that you consider to be relevant? Please give examples.

7. How would you rate your overall experience during your reading?

Excellent	Good	Satisfactory	Needs Improvement	Poor
1	2	3	4	5

8. How likely would you be to return to me again for another reading?

Definitely	Very Likely	Somewhat Likely	Unlikely	Very Unlikely
1	2	3	4	5

9. How likely would you be to recommend me to a friend as a reader?

Definitely	Very Likely	Somewhat Likely	Unlikely	Very Unlikely
1	2	3	4	5

10. Please feel free to make any additional comments you believe would be helpful to me.

Summary

Reading for others can be a deeply rewarding experience. It is a ministry, a God-centered service that you, as a medium, bring to other people in order to help them. When a grieving person hears from a loved one in Summerland, the comfort and hope brought by Spirit can give them the strength and the courage to face another day. The knowledge that their special someone is still around and still very aware of life continuing on reaffirms that their love is not being spent in vain. You, as the medium, are the facilitator for this process, and it is a humbling and honorable place to be. Remembering that reading is a great responsibility will enable you to always do your work for others with the best possible intentions.

Conclusion

Where to Go from Here

Let's pretend for a moment that I'm doing a reading for you. We sit together, you and I, in my office. On the low table between us, a candle burns, lighting the sunshine placemat that covers the surface. On this mat, I have turned over a tarot card, one that reveals where you are right now in your life and where you will be going in the very near future. What card is it?

It is Major Arcana card number 13—Death.

You and I smile knowingly at each other over this card. You, being a mediumship student, know what this symbology means. You realize that this is the end of a cycle for you. It is a time of releasing old, outworn ideas and ushering in new, exciting energies. Your way of thinking has changed; you've learned and grown as you've taken up these spiritual studies, and you're no longer the same person you were before. You have embarked upon the most important journey of your life—the journey toward spiritual enlightenment—and now there is no turning back.

I hope this prospect is exciting to you. Maybe you're a little scared. After all, by now you've probably experienced some things that many people in your life would not understand. There are many, many of us, however, who *do* understand, and I pray that you will find some of these people with whom to share your experiences. Mediumship work cannot be done in a vacuum. As much as we can tune in to Spirit to receive guidance in our own lives, the importance of this work and its message bleeds out into everything we do. It colors our perception of life in myriad ways. Once we have connected with Spirit and realize the vast amount of love and knowledge those on the Other Side can share with us, it's nearly impossible not to try to bring these messages to other people.

I hope that your journey through the pages of this book has been meaningful. I hope that you have learned something of value about the spirit world, those in it, and how they communicate with all of us. More than that, I pray that you have learned something profound about yourself and that you will continue your spiritual studies in your quest to know Creator as intimately as possible. Mediumship is one little component of that process; I hope that I have given you at least a tiny glimpse of the possibilities inherent in your own soul.

So where do you go from here? My suggestion, if you are interested in becoming a professional medium, is to study mediumship in whatever way you can. Finding a good development teacher in your area would be an excellent place to start. Try contacting the closest Spiritualist church to ask if they can direct you to a teacher, or inquire to see if their own organization offers classes to seekers. Another option is studying in a mediumship training program, like the ones offered by the Indiana Association of Spiritualists at Camp Chesterfield, Lily Dale Assembly in New York, or my own church, the United Spiritualists of the Christ Light in Cincinnati, Ohio. For more information about these programs and others, please see Appendix B of this book. You can never have too much knowledge, and these types of classes will only enhance your spirit communication skills.

I hope you'll also continue to practice your meditations, the spirit games and exercises outlined in this book, and the reading techniques for others that we've discussed. Constant working will improve your ability to see, hear, and sense Spirit every day. Talk to your guides as you would to your best friends. They are right there next to you, awaiting your call. Know that your spirit loved ones send you high vibrations from the spirit world every day, just as you think of them each day. Remember that love is the greatest force in the Universe, and it transcends time and space.

And so we come to the end of our journey together, you and I. I hope that perhaps our paths will cross again sometime. Until then, I thank you for allowing me to work between the two worlds with you.

Appendix A

The Principles of Spiritualism

1. We believe in Infinite Intelligence.

2. We believe that the phenomena of nature, both physical and spiritual, are the expression of Infinite Intelligence.

3. We affirm that a correct understanding of such expression and living in accordance therewith, constitute true religion.

4. We affirm that the existence and personal identity continue after the change called death.

5. We affirm that communication with the so-called dead is a fact, scientifically proven by the phenomena of Spiritualism.

6. We believe that the highest morality is contained in the Golden Rule: "Whatsoever ye would that others should do unto you, do ye also unto them."

7. We affirm the moral responsibility of individuals, and that we make our own happiness or unhappiness as we obey or disobey Nature's physical and spiritual laws.

8. We affirm that the doorway to reformation is never closed against any soul here or hereafter.

9. We affirm that the Precepts of Prophecy and Healing are divine attributes proven through Mediumship.

(National Spiritualist Association of Churches 2002)

The principles were communicated from Spirit by means of mediumship. The first six principles were communicated in October 1899. The next two were given in October 1909. The last principle was given in 1944 (32).

Appendix B

Spiritualist Organizations in the United States*

Indiana Association of Spiritualists
    Camp Chesterfield
    P.O. Box 132
    Chesterfield, IN 46017
    765-378-0235
    http://www.campchesterfield.net

Lily Dale Assembly
    5 Melrose Park
    Lily Dale, NY 14752
    716-595-8721
    http://www.lilydaleassembly.com

---

*This list is by no means comprehensive and does not include any international organizations. For more information, please contact the organization itself.

The National Spiritual Alliance
P.O. Box 88
Lake Pleasant, MA 01347
http://www.thenationalspiritualallianceinc.org

National Spiritualist Association of Churches
General Offices
P.O. Box 217
Lily Dale, NY 14752
716-595-2000
http://www.nsac.org

United Spiritualists of the Christ Light
4412 Carver Woods Drive, Suite 204
Blue Ash, OH 45242
513-891-5424
http://www.uscl.org

Universal Spiritualist Association
4905 West University Avenue
Muncie, IN 47304-3460
765-286-0601
http://www.spiritualism.org

Bibliography

Angel Focus. 2004. "The Hidden World of Elementals." *Angel Focus* (February 2). http://www.angelfocus.com/elementals.htm (accessed November 24, 2004).

Bethards, Betty. 1983. *The Dream Book: Symbols for Self-Understanding.* Rockport, MA: Element Books Ltd.

Brennan, Barbara Ann. 1987. *Hands of Light: A Guide to Healing through the Human Energy Field.* New York: Bantam.

Cadwallader, M. E. 1917. *Hydesville in History.* Reprint, Lily Dale, NY: Stow Memorial Foundation/National Spiritualist Association of Churches, 1992.

Fodor, Nandor. 1934. "The Ghost Story which Started Spiritualism." In *These Mysterious People.* London: Rider & Co. (Also available on the International Survivalist Society's website at http://www.survivalafterdeath.org/books/fodor/chapter11.htm.)

The Free Dictionary. http://encyclopedia.thefreedictionary.com (accessed November 24, 2004).

Good News Bible: Today's English Version. 2nd ed. 1992. New York: American Bible Society.

Judith, Anodea, Ph.D. 2000. *Wheels of Life: A User's Guide to the Chakra System.* St. Paul, MN: Llewellyn Publications.

Melody. 1991. *Love Is in the Earth: A Kaliedoscope of Crystals.* Wheatridge, CO: Earth-Love Publishing House.

National Spiritualist Association of Churches. 2002. *NSAC Spiritualist Manual.* Lily Dale, NY: National Spiritualist Association of Churches.

RavenWolf, Silver. 1996. *Angels: Companions in Magick.* St. Paul, MN: Llewellyn Publications.

Ryan, Terry. 2000. "Natural Law." Lecture, Indiana Association of Spiritualists.

Spiral Dance. "Glossary." *Spiral Dance.* http://spiraldance.deep -ice.com/glossary.htm (accessed November 24, 2004).

Three Initiates. 1912. *The Kybalion: A Study of the Hermetic Philosophy of Ancient Egypt and Greece.* Chicago: The Yogi Publication Society.

Virtue, Doreen. 2003. *Archangels and Ascended Masters: A Guide to Working and Healing with Divinities and Deities.* Carlsbad, CA: Hay House.

Index

A

After-death communication
(ADC), xviii, 6, 8, 13, 15,
141, 164–165, 208, 211
Afterlife, other names for, 6
Alchemy, 95, 99
Altar space, 81, 204
Angels
Compared with spirit
guides, 115
Guardian angels, 116
Animals
In Native American tradi-
tions, 123, 154
And spirit guides, 6, 123,
135–136, 154
As symbols, 136, 153–155
Archangels, 116, 152
Ascended Master guides
List of, 112–113

Meditation to connect with,
196–198
Working with, 110–112, 151
Auras
Definition, 47
Exercise to feel auras, 48–49
Exercise to see auras, 48
Use in readings, 47, 52, 55

B

Bible, 8, 14, 17, 108, 156,
211–212, 215
Breathing
Exercise for deep breathing,
58
Importance in working with
Spirit, 57
Buddha, 111–112, 196

C

Camp Chesterfield, 13–14, 80, 88, 125, 229, 240
Chakras
  Chart and diagram, 50–51
  Definition, 49
  Quiz, 52–53
  Use in readings, 52–55
Clairaudience, 36–38, 45, 50, 122, 136, 141, 148, 152
Clairaugustine, 37–38
Clairsentience, 37–38, 45, 50, 52, 122, 136, 148, 157, 192
Clairvoyance, 36, 38, 47, 50, 52, 112, 121–122, 136, 151–152, 154–155, 157, 218, 223
Colors
  Of chakras, 49–50, 52–54, 65–67
  And spirit guides, 80, 101, 107, 135, 139, 150, 180–181, 186
  As symbols, 151–152, 172, 186, 190, 192
Concentration, meditations for, 68–69
Creator
  Energies in (male and female), 7, 13
  Loving light of, 42, 65

Prayers to, xix, 119, 204, 215
Terms for, 7

D

Death
  Of a sitter's loved one, 233–234
  As symbol, 187, 239
Discernment, 39–42, 209
Divination tools
  Blessing for, 204
  Cleaning energetically, 205
  Use in readings, 203–205, 214, 226
Doctor chemist guide, 95–99, 108, 118, 123–126, 135–136, 142, 173, 177–178
Doctor of philosophy. See Doctor teacher guide
Doctor teacher guide, 91–94, 99, 101, 108, 123, 126, 135–136, 139–142, 173, 176–177, 185
Dreams and dreamwork
  After-death communcations in, 164–165
  Exercises, 167–170
  About loved ones, 163–168
  Recording, 168–170

E

Earth symbols, 153
Ectoplasm, 98–99
Elementals, 6, 127–128
Energy system, 47–55
Evidence and evidential messages, 219, 229–232, 234

F

Faeries, 6, 128
Fox family (Catherine, Margaretta, Leah, Margaret, John), 9–12
Free will, 13, 16, 40, 85, 214, 227, 229

G

Gatekeeper guide, 140–141, 167, 169, 221
Gems, as symbols, 151
Gnomes, 127
God. *See* Creator
Golden rule, 17
Guided meditations
  Chakra-Cleansing Meditation, 65–67
  Concentration Meditations, 68–69
  Connecting with Ascended Masters, 196–198
  Guide Meditation, 100–101
  Introduction to, 61, 78
  Master Guide Meditation, 109–110
  Simple Protection Meditation, 63–65
  Simple Relaxation Meditation, 62–63
  Special Place Meditation, 70–71
  White Light Meditation, 41–42
Guides. *See* Spirit guides

H

Hermetic Principles, 18
Hydesville, New York, 9

I

Impressional mediumship. *See* Clairsentience
Indiana Association of Spiritualists, 240
Infinite Intelligence, xix, 13, 18
Inner band guides, 77, 118, 127
Intention, setting, 22, 41–42, 124, 233
Internet, 149, 208–209

J

Jesus, 14, 17, 47, 81, 111–112, 152, 196, 211–212
Jewels, as symbols, 151

Journal, for recording and
learning, 25, 29, 42,
48–49, 52, 61, 72, 100,
135–136, 140, 142–143,
145, 149, 158, 160–162,
167–170, 174, 176–178,
180–181, 186, 188–189,
195, 198
Joy guide, 79–83, 99, 101, 108,
123–124, 126–127,
135–136, 139–142,
173–175

L

Law of Attraction, 20–22, 225
Law of Balance, 23
Law of Cause and Effect,
21–22
Law of Compensation, 22
Law of Love, 17
Law of Mind, 18, 21–22
Law of Use, 24
Law of Vibration, 18, 20, 22, 46
Lily Dale Assembly, 13, 240

M

Main message guide, 140–141,
148–149, 157, 161, 179,
185
Master guide, 103–110, 112,
116, 123, 136, 139, 142,
173–174, 196–197
Master teacher. *See* Master
guide

Meditation
Purpose of, 59, 72, 77
Tips, 60
See also Guided meditations
Medium
Definition, 6
Fraudulent, 12, 98
Physical phenomena medi-
ums, 98
Reasons for becoming, xvii,
29, 31–34
See also Readings
Mediumship
Definition, 6
Physical work, 43, 45–46, 55
Reasons for studying, 32–33
Rules of, 39–41, 141, 213
Unacceptable reasons for
studying, 33–34
See also Readings
Merlin, 105–108, 123, 142
Metals, as symbols, 151–152
Mohammed, 8, 111, 113, 196
Murder, of a sitter's loved one,
234

N

National Spiritualist Association of Churches (NSAC),
8, 13
Native American guides,
83–84, 97, 107, 122–125,
136, 142, 154

Natural Law
    Definition, 15
    Underlying principles,
        16–17
    See also Law of Love, Law of
        Mind, Law of Vibration,
        Law of Attraction, Law of
        Cause and Effect, Law of
        Balance, Law of Use, Law
        of Compensation

O

Other Side. *See* Summerland
Outer band guides, 77,
    117–119, 127, 142

P

Pagan, 8
Past lives, 7, 21, 83, 92–93, 107,
    115, 139, 151, 215
Physical phenomena, 98–99
Prayer, xix, 41, 81, 97, 118–119,
    156, 195, 204, 215
Protection, 41, 55–56, 63, 65,
    70, 89–90, 113, 116, 126,
    154–155, 196, 218
Protector guide, 83–90, 99,
    123–126, 135–136, 142,
    175–176
Psychic
    Compared with medium, 5
    Definition, 5

R

Readings
    Addressing fears before-
        hand, 211–213
    Conducting, 87, 203, 209,
        213–215, 217, 225, 233
    "Don'ts," 225–228
    Ending a reading, 235–238
    Evaluation form for, 237
    Identifying spirits in,
        221–223
    Interpreting messages in,
        54, 213, 217–219, 230
    Medical advice, avoiding,
        52, 227
    Mistakes in, 219–220, 228,
        232
    Online, 208–209
    Prayer before, 215
    Starting out, 201–202, 207,
        211, 226, 232
Relaxation, 59, 62–63, 65, 68,
    78, 190, 228. *See also*
        Breathing *and* Meditation
Rosna, Charles B., 10–11

S

Salamanders, 128
Senses, spiritual and physical,
    35–38, 43, 45, 72
Silver cord, 168–169
Sittings
    Definition, 209
    See also Readings

Sleep-state after-death com-
    munications, 164–165
Spirit
    Controlling, 39–41, 101,
        141, 213, 229
    Definition, 7
    Working with, xviii, 5–8,
        10–12, 17, 20, 23–25, 29,
        32–34, 37, 39, 41–45, 47,
        54, 57, 59–60, 69, 72, 80,
        83, 87–90, 92–93, 96–98,
        110–111, 116, 118, 121,
        124, 126, 128, 133,
        135–136, 141–143,
        147–148, 150–152,
        156–157, 160, 171–173,
        177, 179–182, 186–187,
        189, 192–193, 195,
        201–204, 207, 209, 215,
        219–223, 227–228, 230,
        232, 235, 240–241
Spirit communication, 8, 14,
        25, 45–46, 77, 133, 162,
        204, 212, 240
Spirit contact, 5, 208, 228
Spirit guides
    Definition, 7
    Differentiating between,
        123
    Exercises, 81, 99, 157–158,
        160–161, 169–170,
        173–178, 195–198, 220,
        228
    Games, 179–183
Getting to know, 99, 109,
        118–119, 121, 123, 125,
        135, 140, 143, 182
    Meditation to meet guides,
        100–101
    Working with, 5, 7, 12, 47,
        72, 78, 80–81, 84–86, 88,
        93, 95–96, 99–100, 103,
        105, 107–108, 110–111,
        116–119, 121, 123, 126,
        128, 133, 135–137,
        139–143, 147–150,
        154–161, 163, 169–171,
        173–175, 177, 179–182,
        185–187, 189, 195, 201,
        203–204, 208–209, 215,
        217, 219–223, 228,
        230–231, 235–236, 241
Spiritualism
    Centers for, 13
    Compared with other reli-
        gions, 7–8
    Definition, 8
    Origin of Modern Spiritual-
        ism, 9–12
Spiritualists, 7–8, 13–14,
        92–93, 209, 211–212, 229,
        240
Stones, as symbols, 151–152
Suicide, of a sitter's loved one,
        234
Summerland
    Description, 6, 19
    Origin of term, 6

Visiting, 167
Working with spirit people
in, 7–8, 20, 167
Sylphs, 128
Symbolism
Association, 128, 145, 147,
149, 151, 161
Common symbols, 155–157
Consistency in, 147
In dreams, 155, 162,
170–173, 201
Exercises, 149–150, 157,
160–161
Quiz, 189–191
Universal symbolism, 149

T

Tarot, 31–32, 87, 155,
203–205, 214, 239. *See
also* Divination tools

U

Undines, 128
United Spiritualists of the
Christ Light, 240
Universal symbolism, 149
Universe, Natural Laws of the.
See Natural Law

V

Vibration
Law of, 18, 20, 22, 46
Rate of, 19–20, 46, 106–107,
109, 151, 197
Vicarious atonement, 13

W

White Light Meditation, 41–42
Wicca, 6, 14, 32

Free Magazine

Read unique articles by Llewellyn authors, recommendations by experts, and information on new releases. To receive a **free** copy of Llewellyn's consumer magazine, *New Worlds of Mind & Spirit,* simply call 1-877-NEW-WRLD or visit our website at www.llewellyn.com and click on *New Worlds.*

Spirit Guides & Angel Guardians
Contact Your Invisible Helpers

RICHARD WEBSTER

They come to our aid when we least expect it, and they disappear as soon as their work is done. Invisible helpers are available to all of us. In fact, we all regularly receive messages from our guardian angels and spirit guides, but usually fail to recognize them. This book will help you to realize when this occurs. And when you carry out the exercises provided, you will be able to communicate freely with both your guardian angels and spirit guides.

1-56718-795-1
368 pp., 5³⁄₁₆ x 8 $9.95

Spanish edition:
Ángeles guardianes y guías espirituales
1-56718-786-2 $12.95

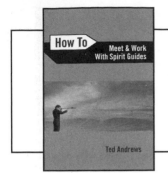

How to Meet & Work with Spirit Guides
TED ANDREWS

We often experience spirit contact in our lives but fail to recognize it for what it is. Now you can learn to access and attune to beings such as guardian angels, nature spirits and elementals, spirit totems, archangels, gods and goddesses—as well as family and friends after their physical death.

Contact with higher soul energies strengthens the will and enlightens the mind. Through a series of simple exercises, you can safely and gradually increase your awareness of spirits and your ability to identify them. You will learn to develop an intentional and directed contact with any number of spirit beings. Discover meditations to open up your subconscious. Learn which acupressure points effectively stimulate your intuitive faculties. Find out how to form a group for spirit work, use crystal balls, perform automatic writing, attune your aura for spirit contact, use sigils to contact the great archangels, and much more! Read *How to Meet and Work with Spirit Guides* and take your first steps through the corridors of life beyond the physical.

0-7387-0812-6
216 pp., 5¾₆ x 7⅝, illus. $7.95

To order, call 1-877-NEW-WRLD
Prices subject to change without notice

Spiritualism & Clairvoyance for Beginners
Simple Techniques to Develop Your Psychic Abilities
ELIZABETH OWENS

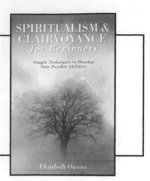

Margaretta and Catherine Fox's successful communication with a spirit entity in 1848 sparked a new understanding of the spirit world in the United States. This new movement is called Modern Spiritualism. Based on Spiritualism's rich tradition, Elizabeth Owens demonstrates how one can develop natural clairvoyant skills in order to hear the "wisdom of the spirits."

Emphasizing patience and practice, the author insists that clairvoyance is possible for everyone. She explains many forms of clairvoyance (psychometry, clairsentience, clairaudience, and so on), and offers examples based on her own experiences and those of six other spiritualist mediums. Exercises in meditation, memory development, visualization, and symbol interpretation progressively help readers enhance and cultivate their own innate gift of the "sixth sense."

0-7387-0707-4
192 pp., 5¾6 x 8 $10.95

To order, call 1-877-NEW-WRLD
Prices subject to change without notice

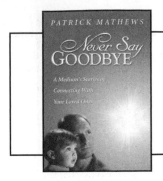

Never Say Goodbye

A Medium's Stories of Connecting with Your Loved Ones

PATRICK MATHEWS

When he was six years old, Patrick Mathews came face to face with the spirit of his dead Uncle Edward. As an adult, Mathews serves as a vessel of hope for those who wish to communicate with their loved ones in spirit. The stories Mathews tells of his life and the people he has helped are humorous, heartwarming, and compelling. Part of his gift is in showing the living that they can still recognize and continue on-going relationships with the departed.

Mathews takes the reader on a roller coaster of emotional stories, from the dead husband who stood by his wife's side during her wedding to a new man, to the brazen spirit who flashed her chest to get her point across. You will also learn step-by-step methods for recognizing your own communications from beyond.

0-7387-0353-2
240 pp., 6 x 9 $14.95

How to Communicate with Spirits
Elizabeth Owens

Nowhere else will you find such a wealth of anecdotes from noted professional mediums residing within a spiritualist community. These real-life psychics shed light on spirit entities, spirit guides, relatives who are in spirit, and communication with all of those on the spirit side of life.

You will explore the different categories of spirit guidance, and you will hear from the mediums themselves about their first contacts with the spirit world, as well as the various phenomena they have encountered.

1-56718-530-4
240 pp. 5³⁄₁₆ x 8 $9.95

Buckland's Book of
Spirit Communications
RAYMOND BUCKLAND

There has been a revival of spiritualism in recent years, with more and more people attempting to communicate with disembodied spirits via talking boards, seances, and other mediums.

Buckland's Book of Spirit Communications is for anyone who wishes to communicate with spirits, as well as for the less adventurous who simply want to satisfy their curiosity about the subject. Explore the nature of the spiritual body and learn how to prepare yourself to become a medium. Experience for yourself the trance state, clairvoyance, psychometry, table tipping, levitation, talking boards, automatic writing, spiritual photography, spiritual healing, distant healing, channeling, and development circles. Also learn how to avoid spiritual fraud.

0-7387-0399-0
272 pp., 8½ x 11, illus. $17.95

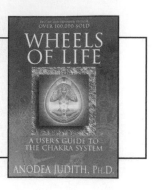

Wheels of Life
A User's Guide to the Chakra System

ANODEA JUDITH

An instruction manual for owning and operating the inner gears that run the machinery of our lives. Written in a practical, down-to-earth style, this fully illustrated book will take the reader on a journey through aspects of consciousness, from the bodily instincts of survival to the processing of deep thoughts.

Discover this ancient metaphysical system under the new light of popular Western metaphors: quantum physics, Kabbalah, physical exercises, poetic meditations, and visionary art. Learn how to open these centers in yourself, and see how the chakras shed light on the present world crises we face today. And learn what you can do about it!

This book will be a vital resource for: magicians, witches, pagans, mystics, yoga practitioners, martial arts people, psychologists, medical people, and all those who are concerned with holistic growth techniques.

0-87542-320-5
480 pp., 6 x 9, illus. $17.95

To order, call 1-877-NEW-WRLD
Prices subject to change without notice

Angels

Companions in Magick

SILVER RAVENWOLF

Angels do exist. These powerful forces of the Universe flow through human history, riding the currents of our pain and glory. You can call on these beings of the divine for increased knowledge, love, patience, health, wisdom, happiness, and spiritual fulfillment. Always close to those in need, they bring peace and prosperity into our lives.

Here, in this complete text, you will find practical information on how to invite these angelic beings into your life. Build an angelic altar, meet the archangels in meditation, contact your guardian angel, create angel sigils and talismans, work magick with the Angelic Rosary, and talk to the deceased. You will learn to work with angels to gain personal insights and assist in the healing of the planet as well as yourself.

Angels do not belong to any particular religious structure—they are universal. They open their arms to humans of all faiths, bringing love and power into people's lives.

1-56718-724-2
360 pp., 7½ x 9⅛, illus. $14.95

To Write to the Author

If you wish to contact the author or would like more information about this book, please write to the author in care of Llewellyn Worldwide and we will forward your request. Both the author and publisher appreciate hearing from you and learning of your enjoyment of this book and how it has helped you. Llewellyn Worldwide cannot guarantee that every letter written to the author can be answered, but all will be forwarded. Please write to:

Rose Vanden Eynden
℅ Llewellyn Worldwide
2143 Wooddale Drive, Dept. 0-7387-0856-9
Woodbury, MN 55125-2989, U.S.A.
Please enclose a self-addressed stamped envelope for reply,
or $1.00 to cover costs. If outside U.S.A., enclose
international postal reply coupon.

Many of Llewellyn's authors have websites with additional information and resources. For more information, please visit our website at http://www.llewellyn.com.